Côte d' Ivoire - Africa

Two battles to win:

"The treacherous Accords,"

&

"Ignorance, [hatred & apathy] at home."

By

Daman Laurent Adjehi

Outskirts Press Inc
10940 S.Parker Road
555 Parker, CO 80134
1888.OP Books
1888.206.8601 fax
www.outskirtspress.com

Cote d'Ivoire--Africa
Two Battles to Win
All Rights Reserved.
Copyright © 2009 Daman Laurent Adjehi
V4.0

French translation by the Author
Cover designed by the Author
Cover photo done by M & M Business Graphics, LLC

Outskirts Press, Inc.
http://www.outskirtspress.com

ISBN: 978-1-4327-2943-1

Outskirts Press and the "OP" logo are trademarks belonging to Outskirts Press, Inc.

PRINTED IN THE UNITED STATES OF AMERICA

Côte d'Ivoire -- Africa

Two Battles to win

The treacherous accords & *Ignorance* [hatred and apathy] *at home*

QUOTE: I heard over and over the following maxim:

"EDUCATION IS THE KEY"

And now, I have begun to question, and doubt its application in Africa. However, knowing within me that this is true, why would a mother [Mama Africa] continue to weep day and night over her slain children and famished progeny? And strain to cope with the scourge of "illiteracy," and the consequences of ignorance? When she can proudly affirm being mother to many educated, talented, and skilled sons and daughters. Why is it that the education of her children is not the "KEY" to her prosperity today?

Daman Laurent Adjehi / Author

Notes: Rebellion is not meant to negotiate with. It is the system by which the colonizers have economically weakened Africa; and are successfully plundering the resources of the continent. The African nations need to truly unite in order to get rid of rebellion, just like when a demon possessed subject is set free.

- He who strikes and fails, and destroys so many lives and dooms a whole nation has no cure for the survivors in any way shape or form.
- The Ivorian people can woefully dwell in this plight of uncertainty for many more years if they reckon on the jaundiced peace-process, all its organizers and advocates. Who is man to rely on him?
- Peace and Sanity are not fruits of the power of darkness; instead, they derive from the Power of Light. The kind of peace that is implored in Côte d'Ivoire is conditional, targeting only one subject.
- The presence of 4000 UN, and 7000 French troops altogether, even of a Million of them, is obstinate, and is likely to produce chaos than a solution to the crisis in Côte d'Ivoire. Their tenure has been controversial to the crisis, and punitive for the agonizing population.
- Which civilized country on earth, in the condition that Côte d'Ivoire is would even use the word "Election" as a mere topic of conversation? First thing first, by priority, then move to the next, and the world will testify how devout and righteous a man you are.

Contents

Contents

Acknowledgements:

THANKS TO FATHER GOD, and my **Lord** and **Savior Jesus Christ** for inspiring me, and calling me to write this book in a short span of time.

TO:

HIS EXCELLENCY, **PRESIDENT LAURENT GBAGBO**, President of the Republic of Côte d'Ivoire. May the Mighty hand of our Lord Jesus Christ continue to be upon you. No one else would have survived all the abuses, and treatments you went through since September 19th, 2002, if it wasn't that God anointed you in a special way to lead your people out of bondage. Côte d'Ivoire is standing today because of your patience, tolerance, integrity, and more so, because you fear God; *Just like King Hezekiah, you agreed to humiliate yourself for the sake of retrieving peace in your country. Keep standing firm, the Lord is with you.*

HIS EXCELLENCY, **PRESIDENT THABO MBEKI**, President of the Republic of South Africa. Excellency, The role God chose you to play in the midst of the crisis in Côte d'Ivoire is priceless. Your reward will come from above.

To:

All the Leaders around the world who have taken the sufferings of the Ivorian people to heart. We highly value the tremendous efforts you have been making in the resolve of this crisis in Côte d'Ivoire.

Acknowledgements:

To:

MY BROTHER BLE GOUDE, and his fellows the patriots; Côte d'Ivoire is proud to have you as her sons. Putting your life on the line to defend your country is a virtue. *You are like the children of Israel who shouted and sounded their trumpets to crush the wall of Jericho, and like the 300 men of Gideon who delivered their nation from the hand of the Medianites and the children of the East.*

All the fallen martyrs, From Emile Boga Doudou, Minister of Interior of Côte d'Ivoire; General Robert Gueï, Leader of the Military Transition in Côte d'Ivoire, and family; Yacé, to the unknown; *your life is not wasted, and you will never be forgotten. You paid the price for the freedom of more generations.*

Dr. Alafuele M. Kalala, President – Rally for a New Society (RNS) and Presidential Candidate in the Democratic Republic of Congo (DRC)

Acknowledgements:

For their special contributions

NAMRUF PRODUCTION, the African Media Network. Furman BARNES,

Faustine Amara Onwuneme, **Editor, Adviser**, in Detroit.

Elvis Halloway. Writer, and Poet, from the Republic of Sierra Leone, in Washington DC.

The family of Papa Kwezituka Mathieu, in Washington DC, Journalist, Writer, and Diplomat from the Republic of Congo (DRC)

Dr. Jose Zephyr. From Haiti- in Washington DC.

Dr. Eric Eddy, Professor at Temple University in Philadelphia, PA.

Sam Mark, M & M Business Graphics, LLC,

Phil Nomel, SR. Editor in Chief, Ivoire Forum

Michel Kassi, English Teacher in Côte d'Ivoire.
Now in Washington, DC; **Proof reader, and editor**.

Haywood Donerson, **Public Relations Agent**.
www.donersonreedgroup.com

Yolanda L. Bynum, **Publicist and Consultant**
www.dreamsandvisionmm@yahoo.com

Pascal Kibissingo, from DRC, in Oregon, USA.
Proof Reader/and my Webmaster.

Acknowledgements:

Special thanks to:

THE FOLLOWING COUNTRIES: for vetoing the constitutional coup d'état of France in Côte d'Ivoire, through the French resolution 1721, at the UN on September 1st, 2006.

1- The United States of America:
    The UN Ambassador: **John Bolton**
"This resolution is affecting the sovereignty of Côte d'Ivoire."

2- The People's Republic of China:

3- Russia:

4- The Republic of Tanzania

5- Japan:
    The UN Ambassador: **Kenzo Oshima**, the Council President for October.
    "There is not going to be a power vacuum in Côte d'Ivoire."

6- The Republic of South Africa:
    The UN Ambassador, **Dumisani Kumalo**.
    "They would never do that to a European country."

7- England:

8- Malawi:

Preface

I WANT TO TAKE THIS MINUTE to thank and praise the Lord for inspiring me to write this small book in a short span of time, and for guiding me throughout this venture. God Almighty is the source of knowledge; and wisdom begins at the fearing of God.

The Lord's mighty hand had always been upon his people: (the Ivorian People) and their country since the invasion of the Midianites and the children of the East. No wonder why all their works have proven fruitless each time.

Since the coup d'état of 1999 that pushed President Henri Konan Bédié out of office, we have experienced several coups attempts, and bloody attacks, but amazingly, the attackers have never succeeded in reaching their goal.
Even when they were undoubtedly sure to succeed and take control, they still failed. This is to me a clear indication that God is in control in Côte d'Ivoire, watching over his people. When God is with you; who can be against you? He was with the children of Israel, as he promised to their fathers; **Abraham**, **Isaac** and **Jacob**, and He never failed them.

One day as the city of Dothan came under siege by the host of the King of Syria; the servant of Prophet Elisha came to him saying:
"*Master, behold, an host compassed the city both with horses and chariots. My Master! How shall we do*? "
"*Fear not; for they that be with us are more than they that be with them.*" Prophet Elisha responded to him, and he lifted up his eyes and prayed, saying, "*Lord, I pray thee, open his eyes that he may see.*"
And the Lord opened the young man's eyes; and he saw: and behold, the mountain was full of horses and chariots of fire round about Elisha. He saw that the army that protected them was bigger and stronger than the Syrians' army.

Preface

So in the case of Côte d'Ivoire, there might be a legion coming against us; but let us not be afraid because the Lord is in control.

The purpose of this book

FOR HIS MIGHTY NAME to be glorified in the midst of this terrible time experienced by the Ivorian people, and Côte d'Ivoire, **in Jesus name**. Yes, many times the children of Israel were torn apart, and afterwards, God restored them again and again, evidently after they had repented and reminded Him of the Covenant that He made with their fathers; Abraham, Isaac, and Jacob – who later became Israel. So Côte d'Ivoire will be restored, in the name of Jesus Christ.

Now, let me ask you this question:

Can you as a people of the country of Côte d'Ivoire remind God of the covenant he made with your father?
Or fathers? We all know that this nation, Côte d'Ivoire had a father as well, known of everybody. If yes, let us say Amen. Otherwise if the answer is no, then let us all, the children of God in this nation get together and make a new covenant with our father in Heaven. Since we have been born again, let us join hands and do it so that in later time, our children and grand children will remind God of the covenant he made with us, their fathers, should trouble come their way. So I urge all the men of God in this country to truly seek the face of the Lord, because if Cote d'Ivoire is still standing, it is because of you, and your continuous prayers.

We thank all the countries, people, and Leaders around the world who got seriously and honestly involved in the resolve of the crisis in Côte d'Ivoire. We gratefully value the tremendous efforts they have made in preventing the diplomatic coup d'état instigated by Jacques Chirac, Kofi Annan, and the Ivorian opposition, against President Laurent Gbagbo of Côte d'Ivoire. The whole world is

Preface

astonished, and the gang of our enemies is troubled after the failure of their well crafted coup against President Laurent GBAGBO. They are so caught unawares that they are almost losing it. You can tell by hearing their hypocritical requests, and provocative comments everyday. They are far from comprehending why this is happening to them. Since they do not know God and the word of God, they will remain in confusion forever.

We, children of God know that every war is spiritual, and every victory is divine. In the book of **Exodus 17: 8-12** when Amelek came against the children of God, Moses told Joshua to choose men of valor to confront Amalek in the valley, while he went on top of the mountain.

You can see that Moses had his arms lifted up, interceding, and every time he became weak and lowered them the enemy seemed to overpower Joshua. But when he picked up strength and raised them again, Joshua overpowered Amalek. So Aaron and Hur stood on each side of him, holding Moses' arms, while he sat on a rock, until Joshua prevailed, and defeated Amalek.

Also the wall of Jericho was never brought down with demolishing machines. It came down, crushed at the sound of trumpets and shouts. So, all these episodes help every child of God to understand that victory is detained by God.

God has used this crisis to reveal the destroyers of Côte d'Ivoire, uncover the real enemies of the country, and unite the Ivorian people.
Adversities always have a way of uniting disaffected people, and this is very much evident in Côte d'Ivoire since the crisis broke out. Unity is the most effective problem solving tool.

The first enemies of Côte d'Ivoire are some of the country's own children. They couldn't forever conceal their evil acts. Right after the failure of the coup d'état against President

Preface

Laurent Gbagbo, they have all converged in one group, under the name of G7; thus making an alliance with the rebels. Concerning this kind of association, the BIBLE teaches us that when a person is possessed by a demon, and that demon is cast out, he goes and fetches seven other demons stronger than the original; and together they come back to attack. When they succeed in taking possession, they make the case of the oppressed person worse. Considering Côte d'Ivoire as a person under demonic pressure, it was first attacked by a legion. And when this legion was cast out and sent in the wilderness, came in the sponsors for whom they were running the errands, the 7 goliaths as a back up. They are as follows:

1- Alassane Dramane Ouattara,
2- Wade,
3- B. C,
4- A.T.T,
5- The colon Chirac,
6- PDCI,
7- RDR and some opposition parties; as described by Jeune Afrique the intelligent (**J.A Intel**) of **11/21/2005**.

Foreword:

For the evaluation of the crisis in Côte d'Ivoire, we will follow four assertive directions: **1**-the cause of the crisis, **2**-the behavior of individuals, **3**-the solutions to the crisis, and **4**-the spiritual aspect of the crisis.

1- The cause of the crisis:

A once peaceful and prosperous country is now straining to cope with a hollowing crisis after a foiled coup d'état on September 19th 2002, in the attempt to overthrow President Laurent Gbagbo. Since that day, not only the country has been divided in two, but the Ivorian opposition at large has formed an alliance with the attackers, the rebels who are controlling the Northern part of the country, and the government, the Southern part. This scene is the expression of hatred that the Ivorian politicians have paraded against President Laurent Gbagbo, a brother, not an intruder. For personal interests, people make all kinds of alliances, and devise plans to inflict chaos on their own countries. The Ivorian politicians brought this on their own country in the intent to get rid of President Laurent Gbagbo, with the political as well as financial support of their former colonizer. **That was the cause of the crisis**.
For any country to prosper, it needs peace and freedom. That is why, throughout this book, we are going to vehemently condemn all that constitutes an obstruction to peace and freedom. For the welfare of our countries, and the wellbeing of our populations, we need to strive for peace and freedom, and oppose to any negative and destructive phenomenon such as: coup d'états, rebellion, genocide, etc. and all that derives from the power of darkness.

2-The behavior of individuals regarding the crisis:

God, maker of all things instituted the freedom of choice. Every individual is entitled to make choices freely based on his or her own conviction. Whether bad or good the choice you make in life has a price to it. Who are we to judge or condemn someone for making his or her own choices? Note: there are two major aspects that need to be taken into consideration while we are making choices:

Foreword:

A) The personal interests.
When you make a choice, you need to know that you will pay the price that comes along with it. When the choice is wrong, you can only blame yourself for the consequences.
B) The interests of significant others.
When the choice you make endangers the lives of your children and significant others, that is when a problem arises. At that point only, you will be judged, talked about, and be blamed or praised in some instances. We are in this predicament today because some people made the wrong choices that have endangered the lives of many. As a result of that, there is today a high level of frustration and anger in Côte d'Ivoire. Therefore, the comments we are going to make concerning the whole crisis may sometimes be harsh. Regardless of such comments, and views, the common denominator is that we should all seek solutions to bring back peace and freedom, and strive to normalize the situation of our country.

3- Solutions to the crisis.
How beautiful it is for brothers and sisters to dwell together? For nearly five years now we have not found a solution to this crisis after all the efforts that have been made since day one. The reason why we have not moved a step forward is that there are too many personal interests involved. More than ever, the country is calling upon each one of us to rise above our personal interests, and rather look at the beautiful country we have, and all the potentials and opportunities we are missing today. Let us give answers to these two questions: **a)** what have you gained by keeping your own country hostage? **b)** What if you let go your ego, and turn round, throw your guns away and meet your brothers and sisters half way, wouldn't you feel happy after all? Remember that a kingdom divided against itself never prospers.

4 –The spiritual aspect of the crisis.
Every situation that occurs in life has two aspects to it: **a)** The physiological, or physical aspect, and **b)** The spiritual aspect.

Foreword:

Concerning the crisis in Côte d'Ivoire, we are following step by step the development of the physical side of it, and we see the dishonesty, the plot, and the skim of destabilization of our country. Because of the above mentioned facts, all the accords, the meetings, the sanctions, and the numerous resolutions have brought little in terms of resolving the crisis and unifying the country. Nevertheless, above all, there is the spiritual aspect of it; the **Will of God** in this crisis. Besides this, everything else is vanity. All will pass away; including the killers, the plotters, the guns, and the mortars, even the flooded bank accounts, with the money stolen from us; but what will remain is: the **Word of God**. May his will prevail in the midst of the crisis in Côte d'Ivoire.

Introduction

I **HAVE BEEN CALLED THIS DAY TO ENGAGE** another aspect of the battle for the liberation of our country, Côte d'Ivoire in particular, and Africa, our continent in general. As I was growing up, I learned through experience that freedom is the greatest attribute of mankind. No one has the right to deny it, or to conceal it from he who yearns for it. As much as it is important for human's individual growth, freedom is essential for the total development of a country. Developed countries have simply taken advantage of the privileges of freedom to research, create, build, and set themselves at the level of autonomy and control. On the other hand, third world countries have been denied the same freedom, so they are unable to fully embrace the chapters of development. They even have the raw materials but they can not set the sale prices for them. Instead, the buyers impose their own prices; the lowest possible to make the African people feel worthless, and keep them poor with their products, while it should be the other way around. And afterward when the finished goods are brought in our countries with the price tags, the cost is outrageous. For almost a half century, all the products of African countries were declared a property of the colonizing countries; and they still are. Even with the declaration of independence, the colonial contracts were still in full force, oblivious to our populations.

Today I urge every soul and mind to look at the continent of Africa, and try to find the answer to the following questions: Why does the continent of Africa have all the resources in its belly, and

Introduction

all the manpower, and still is called a third world continent? All the resources that have been extracted and exported for a half century, what have they served for? Why the blood of the innocent African children is shed everyday? So seeing our continent, Africa in general, and our countries in particular still oppressed and still living under the clutches of colonial rules in this new millennium, is not acceptable. I feel that I should address this issue boldly at the best of my ability. Though no one is perfect, some people may get offended by reading what they did not want to hear; (the truth); if such is the case, my apology. In the same token, I am not writing this book to please anyone. I am addressing an issue that is real, tangible and so crucial that it has virtually deteriorated the image of the motherland.

Africa is known as a land imbued with all imaginable resources; natural and mineral, which God made available to human. A land with a people ingrained in a variety of cultures, where wisdom is almost like a religion. Africa is a land embedded with all the precious items, but still poor; a land that needs help, for the continent has suffered for so long from the plaques of colonial abusers; from human trade, to the plundering of our resources. For Africa to get out of the third world perimeter and be free to develop itself with its own resources, without even outsourcing, two things must happen: **1- colonialism must die,** and **2- patriotism must kick in**.

So my reason for writing this book does not solely repose on the topics of the disarmament of the rebels in Côte d'Ivoire, and the unification of the country; or who should exercise the executive power between the elected President, and the Prime Minister whom he appointed by decree. But, to raise and highlight the most crucial, and alarming issues that shape the social, economic, and political welfare of Africa.

I am assessing these issues with a significant amount of personal experience and exposure that have bestowed on me useful perspective into the troubling tissue of "Hard Core" politics and governance – experience that has instilled in me tremendous

Introduction

judgment to take on the plagues that have dealt a perennial fissure on the integrity of Africa.

In the prospect of the plagues that haunt Africa, Côte d'Ivoire became the new target of an elaborate and international conspiracy targeted at President Laurent Gbagbo and his government. Amazingly, the coup d'état failed, and the scheme of destabilization was unveiled. As a result, and in spite of the failure of the plot, the country took a sharp blow that kept it in an unstable condition.

Although in the history of Côte d'Ivoire, we had our share of down times that we recalled sometimes, but **September 19th 2002** was unlike any other moment.

I would describe that day as "**the day of jubilee**" for our enemies and the assailants, because:

1- They were heavily armed.
2- The national army was under equipped, and unprepared.
3- The President was out of the country, on an official trip to Italy.
4- The Ivorian people were caught asleep; 3:00 AM. The country was in such a state of vulnerability that it did not require much effort from the traitors to subdue the government, and the army.

The itinerary of the rebels in Côte d'Ivoire.

The rebels regrouped and trained for many months in neighboring Burkina Faso, oblivious to the Ivorian people. Anonymous channels broke the iceberg at numerous occasions, but the Ivorian government took the informants as hawkers, and did not act upon the information. **On September 15th**, the rebels invaded the Northern region of the country, and got support from the local population when they revealed their plan of attack. They remained on the Ivorian soil for days before the insurgency, without feeling worried. During that time, they recruited many of the local youths and equipped them. On September 19th, a little after midnight, they launched the attack on the population, while

Introduction

many rebels had already infiltrated Abidjan. In the capital, they hit their first targets successfully, but when it was time to capture the Radio and TV Stations, the local army intervened and confronted them, thus aborting the coup d'état against President Laurent Gbagbo.

The Ivorian people were taken unawares, and left in a state of bitter agony from the time they awoke in the morning. On the other hand, neighboring countries, not only knew about the scheme of toppling President Gbagbo, but were propitious to the project. Many of them contributed one way or the other to protract the sufferings of the Ivorian people. After the dirty war that President Gbagbo fought successfully on arrival, began the strenuous, tiresome and fruitless marathon; from Lomé, Republic of Togo, Marcoussis (France), Accra, Tripoli, Abuja, New York, Addis Ababa, and Ouagadougou. We could not expect more from those numerous meetings than the noticeable attitude of procrastination, as if we asked the devil to cast out demons from an oppressed subject. The only thing we cherished was the extension of President Laurent Gbagbo's term, and the postponement of the Presidential Election from October 31st 2005; to October 31st, 2006, and now October 31^{st,} 2007 by the joint decision of the UN, and the AU.

Well informed Africans know that what transpired in Côte d'Ivoire on September 19th, 2002 goes beyond the fact of getting rid of the rebels and having Presidential Elections, or even transferring the Executive power to a Prime Minister who was never elected. That is irrelevant. One thing that I need to clarify here is that the Executive Power is not for sale, neither transferable, nor negotiable. It is acquired through the expression of the voting rights of the population. If it could be obtained any other way, voting rights would never have been instated. But sadly, the experts in public law are insisting that this theory of trading the executive power must be imposed on President Laurent Gbagbo; him alone, knowing that no where in the world has this ever been implemented. Eventually, in their search for solutions to

Introduction

destabilize our country, they came up with the idea of suspending our constitution, the very symbol of the sovereignty of our country. To me, choosing a leader in this 21st century should not create a problem because evolution of time is symmetrical to mental evolution.

DURING THE PRIMITIVE or remote times, if we recall, populations fought tribal wars over limitation of territories, and mostly issues related to kingships. These wars were evidently a proof of supremacy and power. Mankind was mentally alienated, so wars were the prime recourse of solving conflicts, especially among nations. Peace talks were seldom. Today the world has evolved; mankind as well. Dialogues and peace talks have superseded the primitive means of resolving conflicts. Globalization and interdependence are effective ways to respond to the shortages of food and water, and any other crisis encountered by the human race. Technology is playing a major role in the emancipation of mankind and problem solving. Therefore, choosing a leader for any country should be the demonstration of mental and intellectual power. Dialogues and debates should set the records straight, rather than the demonstration of gun power.

[*Even a fool can pull a trigger to commit the most senseless crime.*]

History bears testimony that our continent, the motherland of all blacks, called Africa, even though rich in all imaginable resources; from natural, mineral to human, is facing real issues that need to be addressed aggressively, and globally. Instead, the African people tend to concentrate their efforts on the sporadic uproars that arise here and there in the countries; thus they are unknowingly driven away from the main issue of making plans to take Africa out of the colonial era, and the darkness of ignorance.

The African people have lost their focus on the big picture, and each time that a problem occurs in a country, they are

Introduction

narrowed down to a picture of individualism. This continues to make the conflicts in the continent difficult to assess. The looters of the continent then take advantage of the fact that there is no real unity among African nations and people, and create confusions, then install thieves in order to serve their purpose. While the people believe that they are opposed to each other and continue to fight among themselves, the looters come in to pretend they are helping to settle the conflicts, and take what they can take. The longer the conflict lasts, the more profitable it is for them.

African countries have been dealing with such kinds of conflicts on individual levels for so long that, now, it looks like things will never get better. Consequently, as long as each country will continue to be singled out, like Côte d'Ivoire is at the present time, and they will fail each time to look at things on a broader scale, the continent of Africa will forever remain a desolate place. In order to prevent our continent from becoming a desolate place, we need to identify the problems, the destroyers and their motives, and then contend them once for all. Until then, the world will never understand that we, African people deserve freedom and peace on our land.

THE POINT I AM TRYING TO MAKE here is that, whatever problem we are encountering in Côte d'Ivoire has already been encountered by every French speaking country on the continent. And as we take on the analysis of the events, we discover that it is virtually the same pattern of attacks and slogans used everywhere. This leads us to conclude that somehow, it must be the same predators pursuing to plunder our wealth. And in the process, they are using the same techniques consisting of opposing the populations against themselves in each country of the continent. So they pour machine guns into our countries from their remote locations, across neighboring frontiers. And they hand those guns over to groups of idiots who are desperate in life and power hungry; asking them to make up excuses to justify their act of killing the innocent population. **These idiots then start burning**

Introduction

villages, looting, killing babies who can not even express themselves; mutilating some of them, raping every female on their way, including pregnant women. They slaughter innocent people who have nothing to do with politics, thus tearing down our continent.

And in the end, you ask yourself; aren't these people from this country? Why are they killing their own brothers and sisters? What did the poor population do to be killed?

What is the real motive behind all this? Seeing those killers running with bare feet in the bushes with such eagerness, you ask yourself; who are they chasing? And why are they so angry? Why are they pouring their anger out on the population? The population that is hungered while the men in suits and ties enjoy life and engage in extravagant living with useless expenditures is the same population that suffers when things go sour. It is that same innocent population that pays the price for something it did not do. Why that?

A typical example of such practices is the events that took place in Côte d'Ivoire on September 19th, 2002, and that led the Ivorian population suffer unprecedented atrocities.

It was not a simple revolt as declared the French President Jacques Chirac, but a real war. It was a whole army that came to attack our country. These men were heavily equipped; which leads to one simple question:

How could unemployed people such as (rebels), be able to supply themselves with such deadly weapons if they had not been sponsored and financed by an organized society?

The next day of the attack, and the failure of the coup d'état against the government of President Laurent Gbagbo, left the Ivorian people distraught, unable to find the answer to what had just happened to them. Surprisingly, President Chirac of France rushed to declare the following:

"This war in Côte d'Ivoire is an internal conflict. It is the result of a handful of angry militaries claiming their rights of reinsertion

Introduction

into the national army," he asserted as if he was interrogated. I am sure his inner conscience rebuked him for telling such a lie. Certainly, at the exception of the Ivorian people, Chirac and all our close and remote neighbors knew about the plan of this attack. So by making this kind of declaration, he wanted to portray himself as innocent, and argue that he was not involved in the coup d'état against President Gbagbo. Some local as well as foreign newspapers joined in the game of publicity to justify the attack, divert people's attention from the perpetrators, and traumatize the Ivorian people. It was clear this was a coup d'état perpetrated against President Gbagbo, as the circumstances of the attack were not misleading. Also the behaviors of all our friends, neighbors, and the Ivorian opposition were telling.

The behavior of the Ivorian opposition concerning this crisis is an act of betrayal to their country, and to their fellow Ivorian people. I can understand that a few people unite to form a rebellion over a period of time to make a claim; though illogical and inadmissible, but possible. But to see an entire opposition in the country being supportive of the rebellion, and not having one single party speaking a tongue of patriotism, is just unbelievable. I would describe such behavior as the practice of sorcery which constitutes one of myriad destructive factors that have drained the continent of Africa. Sorcery is the basic fruit of evil from which derive hatred and jealousy that are felt everyday in our countries, cities, and villages, that are making things hard, and life as a living hell. So you can see that satan has been ruling over Africa for so long, keeping such a rich continent in bondage. I wonder if the African people notice what I have noticed; not to exaggerate, but there is more hatred than love; whereas we have seen some ethnic groups viewing themselves as superior than the others, decide to exterminate them.

The day love takes over the hearts of the African people, things such as ethnic cleansings, coup d'états, genocides, and rebellion will be heard less and less in our countries.

Introduction

In bad times such as the time of the attack of September 19th, 2002 on Côte d'Ivoire, the wise thing to do for a President in the predicament President Laurent Gbagbo was is to call one's best friend, or the country's best ally with whom it has been entertaining various and lengthy relations for help. Knowing that President Gbagbo was out of the country at the time of the attack, it was compulsory for him to talk to the country's best friend (France) for assistance. He was convinced of knocking at the right door. When he did, the answer he got looked almost like getting slapped in the face. No one would have ever thought that our so-called best friend and long time ally (France) would betray us when we most needed help. The President of France, President Jacques Chirac gave excuses: "No, France can not interfere in an internal conflict such as this. Also you need to know that France does not have a military agreement with Côte d'Ivoire. The only makeshift accord that existed was to assist President Houphouët Boigny and his family, to help them reach a safe heaven in case of danger. So you see; there is nothing I can do. Now, as a friend, I can help you personally; so come here in Paris, and I will guarantee your safety and make sure that your family follows you, because the country is burning. I don't think it is safe for you to go back," President Chirac said to President Laurent Gbagbo.
"Is it true that there is no military agreement between our two counties?" President Gbagbo asked President Chirac.
"Exactly; like I said, the agreement was to help Houphouët and his family," President Chirac replied.
"Ok, thank you for informing me. By the way, thank you for your kindness and your concern for my safety, but I am going back home. If my country is burning, I rather burn with it." President Gbagbo answered President Chirac.

The attack of September 19th 2002 was a total surprise for the Ivorian people. Even though the economic and social life was not as great as it should be, however, there was no indication of an internal conflict arising in the country at that time. The following days of the attack were devastating and confusing, as some local

Introduction

newspapers termed the attack as a confrontation between the two military generations; the Zinzins, and the Bahafoués, and foreign Medias joined in for more confusion. We almost believed them because we had no previous signs of an ethnical uprising or a tribal conflict. The controversy about all this conflicting development was the aftermath of the attack on the capital, Abidjan. This alone triggered eye openers. I then began to question the explanations of the newspapers. Until that day, the Ivorian people had nothing to lean on as what might have occurred, or what prompted this attack.

On September 20th, the following day of the attack on my country, Côte d'Ivoire, I was still not informed about it. As I came down to the computer room of the Federal Reserve Bank of Philadelphia, where I was working at that time in order to check my e-mail, and read some news from home, I was struck by a front page title: "Côte d'Ivoire has been attacked by rebels on September 19th, 2002." So I opened the page to read the content.

"The Interior Minister, Mr. Boga Doudou was killed, along with Robert Gueï and his family. The president was out of the country at the time of the attack.

In addition, many Ivorian people were killed in the process. The criminals attempted to take the TV and the radio stations, but they were pushed back by the local army. A war had been declared and our army, even though under equipped, was fighting to save the country. They fought against a group of rebels mainly composed of different nationalities, including some Ivorian people. The coup was so well planned that they hit the right targets," said the paper.

I was devastated when I read the news. The only thing that came to my mind was: *"these people knew that the Minister of Interior, Emile Boga Doudou was the right hand man of President Gbagbo, and the brain behind the re-foundation program of the FPI. He was killed for that purpose. As for General Robert Guei, he was killed out of vengeance for something he did during the transition period."*

I could not think clearly at that hour to even try to understand or

Introduction

make sense out of what had just happened to our country. It took me a few days to come up with a counter reasoning compared to what President Chirac termed as an "Internal conflict," and what some newspapers defined as a confrontation between the Zinzins and the Bahafoués. I said to myself: "I heard thousands conflicting explanations; from the saying of the President of France, Jacques Chirac, to the comments of local as well as international Newspapers.

I need to get to the bottom of this matter and define the causes, and all the people involved in this genocide. We need to assess **what** happened, **w**hen it happened, **w**hy it happened, **w**here it started from, and **h**ow it all came about?"

What happened? The attack on Côte d'Ivoire, and the atrocities of **September 19th, 2002** could be classified as genocide, because of the intensity of the affliction. It was originally a coup d'état that failed, and turned into a rebellion.

How did we end up into rebellion? Had this coup been successful, there would never have been a rebellion. So the idea of [an internal conflict] as stated by President Jacques Chirac was out of question. It was a replica of what had already happened in each and every French colony. So this was not new to the African people. The tragedy was that the only country left in the region had finally been hit, falling under the same strategy of attack. Unlike the African scenarios, the failure of the coup in Côte d'Ivoire was never an option.

The Ivorian army even though under equipped, was able to push the assailants back to the Northern part of the country, where they settled their stronghold ever since, with Soro Guillaume as leader. Soon after their defeat and settlement, President Jacques Chirac of France invited all the parties involved in the crisis, to meet in France for an attempt of resolve. Leaders around the world through various organizations got involved as well, in order to find a solution to the crisis in Côte d'Ivoire. The Ivorian delegation and all the parties went from Lomé, Republic of Togo, to France where

Introduction

President Jacques Chirac had already drafted an accord named Marcoussis. Marcoussis proved to be another coup d'état rather than a solution to the crisis. After Marcoussis, all the parties came back to Africa, and meetings of Accra I, and II, Tripoli, Abuja, and Addis Ababa were organized under the watch of the African Union (AU) and the ECOWAS. Numerous resolutions and accords were signed during all these meetings and peace talks. They all proved to be a failure in the resolve of the conflict. Although these various meetings had brought nothing to Côte d'Ivoire, and have been a waste of time for the Ivorian people on one hand, the length of time has helped us determine the criminals and the enemies of Côte d'Ivoire on the other hand.

Africa

AFRICA WAS NOT THE ONLY land in the classification of third world countries. The other teammates have long gone out, shaking off the mud; but the continent of Africa, with all the resources in its belly, is still stuck in it, lingering with Francophony. We need to ask ourselves why, in this 21st century, Africa is still a third world continent? One of the many hindrances to the advancement of the continent is the idea of Francophony.

Francophony is meant to indefinitely keep the African countries under the rules of servitude, thus promoting poverty and misery. One of the objectives of Francophony is to reinforce the colonial contracts now called: accords of cooperation between France and all the French colonies, including Côte d'Ivoire. Through these accords, all the resources of those countries or colonies are declared the property of France. In this condition, how can a country develop itself when all its resources are a property of another? How can such a continent get out of the Third World condition and embrace development? I was amused because the 2005 meeting of Francophony was held in Burkina Faso; a poor country that needs help, and President Blaise Compaoré probably felt honored to be the host.

Introduction

Speaking of the actual condition of Africa, the downfall of our continent has been the upcoming of a breed of leaders who forcefully came in power to assist the colonizers enforcing oppression in African countries, instead of focusing on ways consisting of pulling our countries up from what has become a chronic underdevelopment. We were blessed to start off with a few patriots who had a clear and comprehensive vision for the welfare of their individual countries, and the continent. But those patriots were merely slain in the attempt to kill and burry their philosophy.

Allow me to use two names as an illustration: **President Thomas Sankara** of Burkina Faso, and **Patrice Lumumba** of Zaire, now DRC. The unfinished work and unaccomplished mission of these patriots will forever indelibly be affixed on our hearts and memories. After these torturous acts of evil, what could we expect from the actors of such a gross usurpation? One came with the wrong concepts. He dwelled on the illusion of immortality, and lured his people into worshiping him at one point. He defied their will and trampled on the very fabric of the Zairians' freedom. He built, and then destroyed what was once their pride. He later died leaving such a courageous people, in the huge and lavishly rich country in an indescribable chaos. The other came to patronize rebellions in the attempt to destabilize neighboring countries. He is very notorious and active in the region; he is one of the strong men to be bound for his preeminent role in the downfall of our country, Côte d'Ivoire, if we intend to heal. Why wasting such precious minds to finally gear our countries in the wrong directions? I feel sorry for the continent. People want the power; they acquire it, and because of bad leadership, have led our continent astray.
I was hoping that Francophony would address and prioritize issues like the economic emancipation, education, security, the bloodshed and all other inhuman conditions that have tarnished the image of our continent.

Let us find answers to the following questions:

Daman Laurent Adjehi - 25 -

Introduction

1- What does Francophony bring to the African countries?
2- Does Francophony provide food for the population? Or:
3- Does it build schools? Or:
4- Does it build hospitals?
5- What about companies to create jobs?
6- Does it address the issues of rebellion, and genocide?
7-What then are the topics of the meetings of Francophony?
I am glad President Laurent Gbagbo did not bother with it, and only sent a delegate. Côte d'Ivoire should get out of unproductive activities at once. The Ivorian people do not feed on Francophony.

I consider Africa as a body composed of several parts that are joined and held together by ligaments, where each part plays a distinct role. When one part of the body is attacked by a cancerous disease, the whole body shuts down, then the person is taken to a physician and an operation is performed to remove the cancer, until the body starts functioning properly. Major surgeries had been performed before: for instance:

In 1957, a tumor of cancer known as colonization was removed from one part of the body called Ghana, and the physician who did the operation was **Dr. Kwamé Nkrumah.** With his peers; people like **Haïlé Sélacié, Aïdjo, Amani Diori, Sékou Touré, Patrice Lumumba**, and many more, they invented a vaccine called: "**Pan-Africanism,**" that was designed to keep the body immune and healthy. Unfortunately though, the vaccine did not get approved at that time because it was too costly. This idea even cost Dr. Nkrumah and most of them their lives.

In 1990, an operation was performed on one part of the body of Africa called South Africa, and the cancer known as Apartheid was removed. The clinic where the patient got admitted was [ANC], and the physician who performed the operation was **Dr. Nelson Mandela**, with his associates: **Steven Biko**, (peace to his soul), **Thabo Mbeki, Oliver Tambo, Bishop Desmond Tutu,**

Introduction

and many more.

Today, I have diagnosed three diseases on the part of the body known as Côte d'Ivoire. The three diseases are: Colonialism, Rebellion, and Ignorance. As a result of this diagnosis, the body of Africa needs to be taken to an emergency room for a major operation. As you can see, history shows that in each French colony, there has been an identical crisis as the one endured by Côte d'Ivoire.

I can assure you that things will never get better in those countries as long as the colonial contracts that bind them to their former master France remain in full force. Bear in mind that France the colonizer will never voluntarily rewrite those colonial contracts to set the countries free, as long as they benefit her. The fact of the matter is that the only country that was left in the region has finally been hit. It was clear President Laurent Gbagbo had been targeted to be thrown out of power. He was being punished for trespassing. He probably did not see the sign that says: [*Do not touch*] on those tattered folders that contain those documents with faded writings; the colonial contracts. As you can see today, no country has been spared in Africa. The problem is so serious that singling Côte d'Ivoire out and trying to unify the country at this point is far from being the solution. This is a global issue that requires a class action in order to liberate all the old French colonies and the whole continent of Africa once for all while the case of Côte d'Ivoire is still current.

There is one and only solution to this matter. We need to take the body of Africa to a clinic called "GOSPEL" where the operation will take place; and the physician who will perform the operation is called "**Doctor** Jesus CHRIST**.**" After the operation is done, while the body is recuperating, we will administer the patient with Dr. Kwamé Nkrumah's vaccine that was discontinued and buried, "the vaccine of Pan-Africanism." After the vaccine gets administered to the patient, there will be a huge transfiguration. As a result, all the resources of the body will be produced, dispatched, and distributed in such a manner that, in places where there is no food, and where babies die of hunger, we will transport food from

Introduction

agricultural areas to supply those areas. In areas where there is no water for climatic reasons, we will irrigate from neighboring rivers and lakes, to supply those dry areas. From places where electrical dams are powerful, we will draw lines to supply dark areas. In areas were education is scarce, we will build schools and send teachers there to teach. We will build roads and highways for accessibility.

We will pass laws that prohibit the proliferation of illegal weapons, and put together a Pan African Army. Wherever we will hear about rebellion and criminals, our united forces will crush it in a matter of days, thus suppressing it. We will no longer have to deal with troops such as Licorne to stop us when we try to take actions to unify our countries in crisis. We will pass laws that encourage entrepreneurship and development programs. We will set the prices of our oil, gold, diamond, and sell them, and with the revenues, we will create opportunities for our children, and develop our continent without the interference of anybody trying to stop us by his influence as a former colonizer, and impose his will on us.

Thus, a major **TRANSFIGURATION** will take place, bringing the motherland up to a competitive level as the rest of the world.

Chapter One
Learning about the attack on Côte d'Ivoire

AS WE LEARNED ABROAD ABOUT the September 19th 2002 attack on Côte d'Ivoire, information revealed that the militants of FPI (the Ivorian Popular Front) which is President Gbagbo's party, from New York and the Delaware Valley; Philadelphia, New Jersey and Delaware were not surprised about this coup d'état that had just been launched. They were more or less aware of a project of destabilization of Côte d'Ivoire, once President Gbagbo would take power.

Prior to the Presidential Election of October 2000, as meetings were held regularly in Philadelphia, Newark, and New York, militants of RDR (Alassane Ouattara's party) would ironically fling at them: "You guys are wasting your time with your numerous meetings; we are collecting money to take the power." It seemed like a joke, but this was a clear indication of what was in preparation. This sarcastic attitude from our former political allies displayed after the dissolution of the [Republican Front]. An alliance which had no republican spirit, but the naivety of one of the allies made it to appear as the solution of the moment when it was formed. The Republican Front was a temporary alliance between the FPI and the RDR at one point, to join forces during the Presidential Elections, in order to defeat the old party PDCI (Democratic Party of Côte d'Ivoire), that was in power for more than thirty years. One would think that the FPI was naïve in the beginning for initiating such an alliance. In the end, the FPI found the necessity to withdraw from the alliance at the right time. This sudden separation allowed each party to show its disposition in the conquest of the power.

The leader of the FPI party (the Ivorian Popular Front), President Laurent Gbagbo knew only one way that leads to power. **"We will be in power one day through election,"** he declared repeatedly even before the campaign.

As a proof, he contended President Houphouët Boigny in 1990 during the Presidential election to tally words with actions. At the end of the day, Houphouët Boigny was proclaimed winner over Laurent Gbagbo because the old man was not prepared to step down and live with the embarrassment. His goal was to die in power like most African dictators. So Laurent Gbagbo backed off as a respectful and obedient son, even though we were all convinced he won the election. After Houphouët's alleged victory, neither the FPI, nor its President ever engaged in unconstitutional or illegal activities; instead, the fight went on. Laurent Gbagbo continued on his non violent and educational trail until the Election Day on October 25th 2000, against General Guei, that brought him in power.

The late Djéni Kobena, former Secretary General of RDR believed in getting in power through election, so he utilized the dissolution of the Front Republican and the rupture from the FPI as an opportunity to prove himself in the conquest of the power. Unfortunately his way of seeing things were contrary to the vision of the party he lead, unknowingly, and this placed him in the wrong place at the wrong time. So he died mysteriously afterwards.

Djéni's sudden cause of death has remained a taboo ever since.

On the other hand, the RDR (Assembly of the Republicans) with its leader Alassane Dramane Ouattara, who became now President of the RDR party, after Djeni's death, chose its campaign slogan, and declared boastfully: "**If we have to walk over the Ivorian people in order to take power, we will. I will also make this country ungovernable if I do not become the President.**"

A real man, whenever he promises to do something, he does it; and whatever consequences derive from such acts, he may assume them responsibly. I wonder why Alassane's followers, the militants of his party, the RDR dubbed him [**Brave Tchê**] meaning [**Brave Man**]. They know that whatever he says he will do, he always does it. And they also know that no one in the country will ever confront him, or the justice system will never question him, as it does to all the bad guys. So he is [ironically] a [**Brave Tchê**]. If someone told you this: "I will set your house on fire." And a week later you see your house in flames as that person threatened you; in this case, what will you do? I guess you will do anything except sitting on your butt doing nothing. Among all, I believe you will first walk to the police station to file a complaint, and then press charges in order to allow the court to investigate to find the arson (s).

But to have a whole country going in flames, blood, and chaos such as this, and not doing anything to find, capture, and bring the perpetrator(s) to justice, is just unexplainable.

Chapter Two

Marcoussis (the plot): **Pr. Mamadou Koulibaly**
The First Lady: **Simone Gbagbo** / Pr. **Laurent Donna Fologo**

Who were the people behind this sinister event?

ONE NAME WAS REVEALED; and it rang a bell. The leader of the rebels was Soro Kigbafory Guillaume. He had a record of being involved in similar activities, perhaps less lethal, but just as *evil* and *inflictive* as the latest.

At the University of Abidjan where he was presumably enrolled in the English department, his true nature revealed itself. He was known to carry machetes instead of pens and pads, terrorizing the whole campus. He was renowned for such activities, so when I heard of him being the leader of the rebellion, I was not as surprised as I would if it was another individual. "He walked his way up," I muttered. How can a nation let such things happen without correcting such an individual? Hearing all he and his gang did throughout the insurgency, I could only put the blame on the government, and the judiciary system of the country. When a person starts acting likewise at an early stage, the Justice system needs to do something in order to prevent the worst. Now it was too late. Soro had grown from a campus disturber to a big time criminal; chief rebel in Côte d'Ivoire. The questions we asked ourselves were: "Did Soro want to overthrow President Gbagbo to take over? Or was he only running an errand for a master? The answer to the question was protrusive. We all know that ambition knows no age, but signs that Soro did not intend to seek power by overthrowing President Gbagbo were apparent. Logically, rebels come to overthrow an existing government, and when they succeed, the chief of the rebels always takes over as the new President until the flames of tension get diffused. In the case of Côte d'Ivoire, I was utterly convinced that Soro was not after the Presidency. I knew he was only an executor, selected by a malevolent society to sweep the way for a mentor who was peering through an aperture from his hide out. Who was he? I asked myself. The answer to that question was yet arduous. Time will tell; I said to myself.

Shortly after the positioning of the rebels in the North, and while the negotiations in Lomé, Republic of Togo were still in session, the Ivorian government received an invitation from the President of France, Jacques Chirac. The purpose of this meeting was to settle, or to find a resolve to the plotted crisis that had been inflicted upon Côte d'Ivoire. At first, the Ivorian people thought that this initiative was to assist the government in its efforts to end the rebellion. When the President of the Ivorian National Assembly, President Mamadou Koulibaly received the invitation of the French Ambassador in Côte d'Ivoire, Gildas Le Lidec, to meet in France, he asked him the following question:

"Is there anything suspicious planned against us that I should know about?" Of course he won't tell you. No terrorist ever reveals his plans of destruction beforehand.

"No, no, there is nothing planned against you. President Chirac wants all of you to come so we can solve the problem," he responded to President Koulibaly.

In President Koulibaly's mind, the French Ambassador's answer was suspicious, but he wanted to grant him the benefit of the doubt.

"What kind of solution does the person who described the war as an internal conflict, have to propose to us? What does he know about this conflict?" So many questions lingered in President Koulibaly's mind. He was right to be suspicious because in Marcoussis, the plot against Côte d'Ivoire was obvious. He noticed two things:

1- The document (Accord of Marcoussis) was written to

accommodate the rebels, and,

2- It was designed to strip all powers from the hands of President Laurent Gbagbo. Marcoussis did not reflect the notion of an accord.

Therefore to me and many Ivorian as well, Marcoussis was void and senseless.

The way Chirac interacts with the African leaders:

Marcoussis was a bombshell and a rip off; therefore inapplicable in Côte d'Ivoire. Things that Chirac would never have accepted, he wrote to impose them on another President. What an animus he holds against Black People? He generally hates blacks, but for the convenience and survival of France, he is obligated to interact with them. For instance, Soro Guillaume and his gang of killers became his trusted associates because he could use them to overthrow President Laurent Gbagbo. He befriends them when he can utilize them as puppies to serve for his purpose of plundering the wealth of the continent. He chose Alassane Ouattara for that reason, knowing that a stranger knows no patriotic virtues. Or an appointed Prime Minister can be given Executive Power ravished from an elected President; as President Gbagbo, because signs of Konan Banny's propensity for the colonial cause bode well. He chases them around to have them killed when they adamantly display maverick signs, and an attitude of non compliance with the contemptuous game of interests, but instead stand for their countries.

President Mamadou Koulibaly, whom I salute here for his courage and integrity, sensed the plot against Côte d'Ivoire since the day he received the invitation to meet in Linas Marcoussis. I congratulate him for leading the delegates of the Ivorian government out of that meeting room in Marcoussis, refusing to accept such a gross humiliation of his country, his President and his people. He had hoped to see something more appealing around that table, instead of what unfolded. President Koulibaly is not only educated, but he is wise and intelligent. He knows the notion of an accord. He knows that when two or more parties decide to enter into an agreement, they sit around a table and write the various clauses of the agreement on the basis that each party gets some sort of satisfaction before ratification. At any given time each party can decide to withdraw from the agreement if they see fit. Marcoussis did not fit that notion. Therefore I would have followed President Koulibaly out of that room, had I been part of the delegation.

Marcoussis was designed for two purposes:

1- To take away all powers from the hands of President Laurent Gbagbo and confer them to the Prime Minister in order to play the role of the President of the Republic.
2- Impose Alassane Ouattara as candidate to the up coming Presidential Election. These two above chapters (1, and 2) portrayed Chirac's deep hatred for our President, President Gbagbo, and his partaking in the coup attempt. As for the chapter (2) alone was enough to nail Alassane to the coup, the killings, and the rebellion without further analysis.

Let us see who Alassane is, and where he came from.

I personally never heard of Alassane Ouattara when I was growing up in my country, Côte d'Ivoire; neither did many of the guys from my generation. In 1989, we were all surprised to hear that Houphouët Boigny, then President of Côte d'Ivoire had appointed a Prime Minister. Who was he? It was a certain man named Alassane Dramane Ouattara; unknown to the Ivorian people; a man with a conflicting background. Alassane Ouattara attended school in Burkina Faso; formerly Upper Volta. There, he did his primary, elementary, secondary, high school and university studies. Who raised him, and took care of him as a child in Burkina Faso? He later traveled to the United States, to Philadelphia precisely in order to pursue further education. Later he worked at the I.M.F as a (Voltaïc) or Burkinabé National. Alassane's educational and professional itinerary revealed that he had neither affective nor biological bond with Côte d'Ivoire in any way shape or form.

It is so true that God can bless anyone unexpectedly, and He can in some instances give the person a whole country for a heritage. With such blessing, the beneficiary can get in a lot of troubles when he later does not follow the principles of He who blessed him. But if the person follows God's principles, and fears Him, he can move from prosperity to prosperity. In return, the inhabitants of that country may welcome you and cherish you as their own. Unfortunately, in the long run, if that person takes their kindness and their love for a weakness, and brings them guns instead of bread, and create conflicting issues such us: *they don't like me because I am a Muslim, and I come from the North*," he can be the cause of the destruction of that very country.

History bears testimonies of religiously related issues that are the cause of endless conflicts around the world.

HOW ALASSANE OUATTARA ENDED UP IN CÔTE D'IVOIRE:

When between the year 1980 and 1985, the economic crisis hit Côte d'Ivoire, and Houphouët contacted the World Bank for help, it happened that Alassane the Burkinabé was the head of the department for African Affairs, and was in the middle of all Houphouët's negotiations with the bank. Before the bank could assist a country financially, the country would have to agree on using its preconceived plan. So Houphouët was compelled to accept any given condition as long as he could get help. However, the plan contained clauses fraught with danger that would hurt the Ivorian people. Among those chapters were: **the privatization of two strategic sectors; the water and electricity companies that were sold to France, and the slashing of the salary of all teachers**. Houphouët himself could not make those extortive and scurrilous decisions without feeling pain in his heart. Therefore, to dull his feelings, and muffle the suffering of the Ivorian people, he needed someone who had no Ivorian blood in his veins to easily impose such grimness on the peaceful Ivorian population. And the Burkinabé Alassane Ouattara was the right pick. This is how Alassane Ouattara landed in Abidjan, with the promise to be granted the Ivorian Nationality while on duty. These measures taken by the new Prime Minister were pretentiously rhetorical, and his nomination was so controversial that the leader of the FPI, the major opposition party at that time, President Laurent Gbagbo could not be silent. He vehemently decried President Houphouët Boigny's violation of the country's constitution for appointing a foreigner. Houphouët then rushed to justify his actions by saying: *"Alassane Ouattara is an Ivorian national. His parents are from the city of Kong, but he was born in Dimbokro."*

As questions begun to outburst irascibly, Houphouët reassures the Ivorian people to remain calm. They relinquished, and went along with his dictum and the event that ensued. They watched tepidly the ceremony of naturalization of Alassane Dramane Ouattara at the Hotel Ivoire, during which Houphouët delivered him a National Identification Card, and a Certificate of Nationality. Many Ivorian people were not excited by the creation of the new [Prime Minister] post, and about the strange man who was brought in to serve as Prime Minister. Instead, they grew suspicious about the whole event, and drew the following conclusion:

"First of all, it is not the President of the nation's duty to deliver documents to citizens. It is every citizen's responsibility to apply for his or her own documents.

Secondly, if Alassane were an Ivorian, why did he need President Houphouët to hand him these documents?

Thirdly, as a citizen of a country, even after staying abroad for many years, the day you return home, you know where you can go to get copies of your local documents. You don't even need to bribe anyone for this. So, regardless of what the President is saying, we know that he is covering up something. He has once again enthralled us. How long will this man take advantage of us?

So let us give answers to the following questions:

1- Suppose Alassane Ouattara was an Ivorian; who were his classmates in the past?

2- At least he has to have some friends of childhood, and throughout the time he was a teenager in high school. Who are they?

3- Did he militate in the school syndicate called MEECI?
4-Which school or schools did he attend in Côte d'Ivoire? 5- At least let us find his High School Sweetheart. If we can't find her, then we have a problem.
The man is a total stranger.
Where was he hiding all this time for him to pop up all of a sudden to be nominated Prime Minister?

Right after the nomination of Alassane as Prime Minister, many, not to say all the politicians of PDCI, the old party in power for thirty three years, literally belittled President Laurent Gbagbo, dubbing him as "*the usual guy who has nothing better to do than whining all the time.*" But soon after, those same politicians (including Bédié) of the old party (PDCI) came in contradiction with themselves. Later when Houphouët Boigny died, and Alassane the Prime Minister grew the desire to confiscate the presidency, they defied him on the matter of nationality, mooting that he was not an Ivorian, and barred him from the race.
For example, at the time of the nomination of Alassane Ouattara as Prime Minister, Konan Bédié (*former President of Côte d'Ivoire*) was the President of the National Assembly. He never uttered a contradictory view to Houphouët Boigny's decision for the nomination; instead he upbraided President Laurent Gbagbo for bellyaching. So when the time came for the Presidential Election, and he was to confront Alassane Ouattara, Bédié became sober enough to argue that: "*Alassane is not eligible because he is a foreigner from Burkina Faso.*"

This is one major inconsistency that I strongly despise about African politicians in general, and Ivorian politicians in particular: *They flow and swing with the wind of complacency. They may say one thing today when it benefits them, and say another thing to address the same issue the next day when it backfires.*
Bédié's argument was true in a sense; but to me, after favoring Alassane's nomination as Prime Minister, you voluntarily gave the man every rights and privileges as a national. Therefore,

you need to fully assume your responsibilities and be consistent all the way. You can not turn around today, because now things do not work in your favor, and tell him he is not an Ivorian. You were wrong in the beginning and you are wrong today. You have fooled not only the Ivorian people, but also yourselves. Remember: you are the worse enemies of the country and its people.

So as an intellectual, Alassane seized the opportunity and constructed his case, substantiating that he was born of a father and mother both Ivorian. There were no laws governing foreigners before the sixties, and there are still none. Also at that time Burkina Faso, formerly Upper Volta was considered the upper part of Côte d'Ivoire, so all the Burkinabés who came in before the sixties can claim they are Ivorian. This in fact would have worked in favor of Alassane Ouattara if he did make sound choices, and bear delightful fruits. Laws are passed, applied and enforced to settle conflicts in life. Also, elections are the only means to becoming the President of a country. Without elections being held, no one can say for sure if he will be voted for, let alone becoming President. Regardless of the ambiguity around his personality, Alassane Ouattara keeps declaring: "I will be President of Côte d'Ivoire," without showing any concern for the sufferings of the Ivorian people. All he is concerned about is "being President." Well, no one becomes the President of any country overnight without proving his eligibility first; making sure that his candidacy can be validated by the Supreme Court, and then tell his constituents the reasons why he wants to be President. At least present a detail program to his constituents, or do something constructive. So, *had I been Alassane; knowing that I am contested regarding my citizenship, I would create an environment such as in the end, I would make more friends. For instance, I would first assess areas of greater needs in the country and start investing in those areas. For example in the capital city of Abidjan, there is a critical and a crucial need for transportation. So I would build a Metro System in the metropolitan area, which would alleviate the nightmare of the residents of Abidjan and surroundings. This investment alone would constitute deliverance for the Ivorian people from their daily struggle. It would also create a lot of jobs for my new brothers and sisters. In the end, the Ivorian people would be the ones to look for me, to include me in the political life of the country.*

Though I am using this as a mere example, I need to emphasize that the Ivorian people are not expecting anything, other than the coups d'états from Alassane Ouattara.

There is a law of nature that people tend to ignore, that is: "when you implement positive endeavors, or give away things that edify, positive things surely come back to you. But when you give away evil, do not expect to shine." Alassane Dramane Ouattara knows within himself that he is not what he claims he is; (Ivorian). And Instead of using a positive way of dealing with the issue, and an intelligent manner to conquer the hearts of the Ivorian people in order to blend in, he has chosen a perverse and malevolent way with intimidating language such as:

"**I will render this country ungovernable**," and

"**If I have to walk over the Ivorian people to get what I want, I would.**" This raucous language does neither reflect intellectualism nor political traits.

A country that is not legally yours; you have to be filled with negative intentions to utter such grating words. One's Intentions can only be known through his utterance. The message was vindictive, spiteful, and coded. It needed to be decoded to know what Alassane Ouattara inferred.

He adopted this arrogant behavior because he knew he had the financial means to carry his plan out, as well as the human resources and political support needed to destroy our country in the process of conquering the Presidency, in case he encountered a hindrance of any kind. This showed that his intentions behind the Presidency were malevolent. It was apparent this man would use the country's resources to pay back his monstrous debts, and sell the country to the highest bidder. Otherwise if his intentions were benevolent, he would have used a friendly language. What more can a normal person want in life? Alassane Ouattara was then given the opportunity to prove that he was the expert he said he was by making miracles in the Ivorian economy. Sadly though, three years at the head of the Ivorian government was proven a scandal and a disaster. The unfortunate thing is that Houphouët, out of all the people he sent to Europe to study, he could not find a qualified person to straighten up the economy of Côte d'Ivoire. And his so-called expert came to worsen the already precarious economical condition of the country.

I am not an economist per se, but to lift up our small countries in Africa, what we need to do is to minimize the useless expenditures, reduce the waste of money to its minimum level, and invest in areas of need and productivity with short or long term turnovers.

Alassane Ouattara mercilessly abused the old man, President Houphouët. He took advantage of his mental impairment to make him sign fictitious agreements, and conflicting documents, among which was a blank check. Only God knows what he did with it, and what the exact figure that he wrote on that check was; and how much billions of CFA Francs he has pumped out into peripheral banks overseas. He claims he is from Kong -- a poor town that needs help from its sons and daughters. Why couldn't he even build it to prove to the Ivorian people that he is indeed an Ivorian, and a patriot?

It came out clearly that Alassane Dramane Ouattara was Chirac's favorite man; according to the spirit of the so-called accord of Marcoussis. . **Let us give answers to two key questions.**

First, what was President Chirac's purpose of drafting Marcoussis? Chirac took his time to elaborate such a raucous document as a solution to end the war in Côte d'Ivoire. Marcoussis was written to soothe the rebels. He unconsciously brought suspicion upon himself as having an important role in the coup attempt against President Laurent Gbagbo. Being on the side of the rebels implied that Chirac, not only knew something about this war, but he was the power behind the coup d'état.

Secondly, what made Chirac call all the protagonists in the conflict to come to France for a settlement, after declining President Gbagbo's request for a military assistance? That was a puzzle that the Ivorian government failed to solve, thus giving power to Chirac to set them up further more.

So far we knew that the enemies of Côte d'Ivoire had failed to overthrow President Gbagbo by night, so they designed Marcoussis to overthrow him by day, rendering him [*persona non grata*].

The road map of Marcoussis was to give executive power to an appointed Prime Minister who would rule the country. Marcousis was not initially the back up plan of the insurgency, because failing was not an option. The accord was written hastily afterwards.

At the meeting in Linas-Marcoussis, all the participants were terribly shocked when President Koulibaly shut the door behind him, leaving the meeting room with the delegates of the Ivorian government. Chirac then drew his claws. Normally a mediator has no rights to get offended in trying to reconcile parties. When one of the parties involved in a particular crisis disagrees on one thing or the other, the mediator has no choice but to make more efforts to find a common point of agreement. But to seize someone by the collars, wanting to fight with him in a mediation process is questionable. Consequently, the French Leaders who organized this latent meeting to further humiliate President Gbagbo, were outraged. They were so out of touch that the French Ambassador in Côte d'Ivoire, Gildas Le Lidec seized President Gbagbo by his collars in his Hotel Room as if he was ready to come to blows with him. In the beginning we thought that President Chirac and his government were only serving as mediators to solve the conflict. Now that the Ivorian Government refused to sign certain contentious clauses, Chirac got offended on behalf of the rebels. What was previously described as **"internal conflict"** had just changed venue.

Up to this point, the picture was still not clear about the role of France in this failed coup d'état against President Laurent Gbagbo. We had bold signs that spoke for themselves. But we needed more evidence though to prove France's involvement and Chirac's responsibility. The Presidency of Alassane imposed by Marcoussis to the Ivorian people was enough to determine at this stage that Alassane himself was linked to the coup and to the rebellion. If Alassane was an Ivorian and a real politician, he would have known that to run for the Presidency, one does not need to take weapons. The procedure is so simple that it does not require bloodshed of innocent people.

We, African people have to join hands and forces in order to change the way we do things in the continent of Africa. Simple things such as (electing a President) that people appraise in developed countries become a nightmare for the African people. Most of the time unqualified and unworthy people, wanting the power for selfish reasons and by any means necessary, have perverted the electoral purpose, and obliterated the sense of the voting process.

Why should we have to deal with grim results such as: orphans, crippled, dead, and grieving families after every election?

We have to make efforts to put an end to these destructive ways in our continent. We have so much educated, talented, and intelligent men and women in every country, capable of reasoning and acting with decency that, to me, *and I am sure you will agree with me*; it makes no sense to still be where we are today. If we all agree in Africa that:

"Education is the Key,"

then we should use our education, skills and talents, to create an environment of prosperity for all; and strive to turn our continent into a land of opportunities, and a bread basket for the rest of the world.

The first Lady of Côte d'Ivoire:
Simone Ehivet Gbagbo

WHEN LATER THE FIRST LADY, Simone Ehivet Gbagbo called to speak to her spouse and see how he was doing, she heard someone yelling in the background, so she asked.

When she was informed about the Ambassador's awkward behavior, she calmly requested to speak to him. When the phone was handed to the Ambassador, she spoke firmly to him:

"*Are you the one making all that noise? Well, you better not touch one single hair on my husband's head, otherwise......We will no longer take your humiliation,*" she warned the Ambassador when she asked the protocol to hand the telephone over to him.

I admire the First lady of Côte d'Ivoire for her courage and her integrity.

I secretly call her "**The Iron Lady.**" Behind a great man, there is always a great lady.

President Laurent Donna Fologo:
President of the Social and Economic Council of Côte d'Ivoire

I RESPECTFULLY SALUTE President Laurent Donna Fologo for his honesty, and his eagerness to bring back peace from every meeting he and the Ivorian delegation attended on behalf of the Ivorian people. From Lomé (Republic of Togo), Accra (Rep. of Ghana), and so on, the head of the Ivorian delegation, President Laurent Donna Fologo believed that he was only dealing with a group of discontented Ivorian militaries. So as a wise man, he thought that solving this conflict would only be a matter of time. In no circumstances, he ever pondered over a plot for the destabilization of his country. Nevertheless, during these meetings, besides the eye catching evasiveness of the African Union in handling the crisis in Côte d'Ivoire, and the display of partiality of the African leaders towards the Ivorian delegation, as opposed to their auspiciousness for the rebels, something bizarre caught his attention. Soro Guillaume the chief rebels requested to use the restroom every fifteen minutes, and during those many breaks, he talked on the phone instead. And as soon as he returned, he asked to speak. He would never make any comment before then. This was a clear indicator that he was briefing one of his mentors about what was being said at the meeting, and that person eventually told him what to say accordingly. Despite this, President Fologo was not deterred. Regardless of whom Soro was reporting to, all President Fologo wanted was peace for his country. It is obvious to be opponents in life and have diverse views; it is the best way to improve in life because one person does not know it all. Therefore, in the event of an attack, you set yours differences aside, come together and fight the enemy. This is the lesson that President Fologo tried to instill in the Ivorian politicians; but they seem not to get it. Obviously, they are not interested in the life of the country. What they are pursuing is the power, and wealth.

"In this difficult time, I need to stand behind my younger brother (President Gbagbo) to fight the enemy together. I cannot turn my back on him," said President Fologo.

Here is a real Ivorian patriot.

While President Fologo and the Ivorian delegation trod on the road in search of peace in the African cities, Chirac hurriedly invited the Ivorian government and the rebels in Paris to implement his diplomatic coup d'état against President Laurent Gbagbo. For most of the Ivorian people, the invitation of Paris appeared to be a breakthrough because France was always considered as ally of Côte d'Ivoire. Consequently, any thoughts of treason by France seemed irrelevant. They thought of everything else except for what took place at the meeting of Marcoussis. In their minds, a scheme of a coup d'état of France, and the idea of wanting to overthrow their President was to be excluded from all topics. But as time went by, they progressively discovered the surprises that France had for them.

"If France has been able to do this to Côte d'Ivoire; Houphouët Boigny's country, this means that France has no regard for us. And from this, we know now that she is the cause of all the troubles in Africa."

Terrorist attack on Prime. Minister Soro's Aircraft:

AS I WAS COMPLETING THIS EDITION, and preparing to launch the book, Soro Guillaume, the chief rebel was appointed Prime Minister by President Laurent Gbagbo, in accordance with the new and final Accord of Ouaga (Ouagadougou). This Accord was the prerequisite of the unification of the country, and the withdrawal of all troops; should they be UN or French. Soro's nomination as Prime Minister of Côte d'Ivoire under President Gbagbo meant two things: **1-** The beginning of peace in the country, and **2-** Treason. This was viewed by his erstwhile associates as a breach of trust. Consequently, while the Ivorian people celebrated a looming peace, and dubbed Soro as a courageous man, he became the new target, and subjected to a terrorist attack; **THE FIRST OF A KIND IN OUR COUNTRY EVER.**

Friday June 29th, 2007. The Aircraft of Prime Minister Guillaume Soro has been attacked by a rocket propelled this morning as he prepared to land at the airport of Bouaké (Central part of Côte d'Ivoire). At least three reported dead and many wounded. Photo: of the exterior of the aircraft that was later brought back to Abidjan Port-Bouët ☛Photograph by: Emma

Chapter Three
Henri Konan Bédié (2nd & former President of Côte d'Ivoire)
His implication in the rebellion

IN 1993, AFTER PRESIDENT HOUPHOUET BOIGNY'S death, the Ivorian people already knew who the next President of Côte d'Ivoire would be. At the announcement of his self-proclaimed Presidency, Henri Konan Bédié made it clear to the Ivorian people: *"From today, I am the new President of Côte d'Ivoire. Therefore, I am asking everyone to be at my disposal."*
In other word, "You, the population have to be ready to serve me. I can care less about you and your children, because you did not put me in power, the constitution did. So do not count on me to solve your problems."

At that time Bédié and all the politicians of Côte d'Ivoire knew the value of [A Constitution] in a country. Before the death of President Houphouët Boigny, he forged the article 11 of the constitution several times before appointing Bédié as the President of the National Assembly, to craft his succession. The article stipulated:
"In case of the absence of the President of the Republic, or in the event that he can not exercise his functions, the President of the National Assembly is to serve as President, at least temporarily, until the next scheduled date of the presidential elections."
So Bédié took advantage of the article # 11 of the constitution to proclaim himself as the new President of Côte d'Ivoire,

superseding President Houphouët Boigny, to finish his remaining two years.

We were all baffled that in 2006, Bédié, the lucky beneficiary of the constitution had formed an alliance with Alassane Dramane Ouattara to have the constitution suspended in order to weaken their brother President Gbagbo, and tie him up. Here are (the selfish) calculations that the Ivorian politicians make. I hate to believe that the former President (Bédié) who should be standing for the strengthening of the constitution did not lose the ability to remember his own history.

When Bédié self proclaimed himself President of Côte d'Ivoire in 1993, the Ivorian people did not react. They conceded and waited to see what he would provide. Obviously they longed for positive changes compared to Houphouët Boigny's scurrilous tenure, such as: a new and perspicuous speech, a new leadership, and a new approach altogether. They hoped that Bédié would be more sensitive to their sufferings. Also they flinched for the respect of the constitution, and for the fact that he was long considered the son of President Houphouët, but especially they recoiled eagerly anticipating some sorts of innovation. In spite of the submissiveness of the Ivorian population, Bédié unfortunately tripped, and grew swollen headed.

For the UN:
"This was an interior affair for Côte d'Ivoire; as long as peace prevails in the country, we are okay."
For France:
"Let us wait and see whether Bédié will be on our side or not. He was a political student of the father; therefore he is likely to assure the continuity of the colonial system. There is no reason why he wouldn't."

Evidently, Bédié assured the continuity by updating the colonial contracts and at the same time served himself copiously, stealing the country blind.

During his Presidency, I never understood his program and development plan. From what he did throughout his time of Presidency, I can deduct that his main goal was to erase the traces and footprints of his father Houphouët Boigny, and then create his own empire. Here is a man who did not suffer to be where he found himself. He became the second President of the country, profiting from the manipulation of the constitution by President Houphouët Boigny. He is the luckiest man to have benefited from the advantages of the old party PDCI, and Instead of reorganizing it and giving it a new direction, and setting fresh goals and objectives, he began to deviate. He simply decided to boycott it to create his own party, C.N.B (Circle National Bédié) as a surrogate to the old party PDCI.

With his idea of boycotting the old party, I do not understand why PDCI is still betting on Bédié. With all the young men in the old party, why clinging to the past? I am baffled.

Throughout the year 1995, the only major activity in the country and for his government was the creation of chapters of CNB. During that time, the majority of the young people were pulled into CNB in such a manner that, I asked myself whether they knew what they were getting involved in. What a tragedy for a student to get involved in something unavailing, or an activity that has no certain future? It is a terrible thing for a student to waste his time and energy on something unproductive, and irrelevant to his future. I knew from the beginning that CNB had no future, and it was only a temporally association. I knew that CNB would not bring salvage to the education or employment needs of all the young people who were drawn in by the thousands. They probably could not understand at that time that they were being used and taken advantage of. I wished I had the opportunity to talk these students out of this mess during my visit to Côte d'Ivoire in December 1995. But when I got to my village, I had the opportunity to pull one of my cousins out after he talked to me about CNB. He was very excited, and I could see the gleam that lit up on his face while talking.

"Cousin, I am the Secretary General of CNB section of this village.

I attend meetings in Divo regularly," he said to me enthusiastically; and I gave him one of those telling looks. I shook my head first, and then I asked him in such a way that he picked up my bitterness about his involvement. "Does the CNB provide opportunities for any aspect of your future such as pursuing further education, getting a scholarship, or getting a job?" I asked him.

"None of these things," he answered me very sadly as if he had just awakened from his slumbers.

"So what are the purpose and the Goals of the CNB, and the reason of your fellowship? What do you talk about during your meetings?" I asked him again. He then looked at me speechlessly. I could see his face frowning like a driver who had just entered into a one way street. He then said to me:

"No, we do not talk about these things. CNB is a club to support President Konan Bédié." The tone of his voice suggested that he did not belong there, and he needed someone like me to pull him out.

"In other words, you are supporting him so he can rule for life. He knows well that if he has behind him all the young people who are of age to vote, he can remain in power for life. Now, do you know that his children are oversees, studying, while some of you have not been to school for sometimes for lack of money? Is he concerned about your future?" I asked my cousin. He shook his head at first, and said to me: "No, I don't think he is."

"Therefore, my advice to you is to forget this and rather concentrate on your future, than wasting your time.

To be honest with you, I can bet you that CNB has no future, and the day Bédié will no longer be the President of Côte d'Ivoire will be the end of CNB. This is how uncertain and ineffectual CNB is. And the way Bédié is governing the country, I can assure you that he will not remain President for a long time," I said to him. During that period, you could not turn on your TV and watch a show without being interrupted for publicity on the creation of a new chapter of CNB. The whole time that I was in Côte d'Ivoire, I was disgusted and traumatized over this. We all know that President Houphouët Boigny worked hard throughout his entire life to achieve that much. At his point of death, he made

Bédié his direct heir, placing on a table before his opponents, a beautiful cake. Instead of acting wisely, and giving to Caesar what is due to Caesar, he simply engaged in the process of "making sure the father died twice and never be remembered." This is one example that when you did not suffer to acquire wealth, you do not value it. Thus, Bédié called upon himself the biggest curse ever. From that point on, he grew from curse to curse. That is why he could not prosper on the father's seat.

The first thing Bédié ought to do for his father as soon as he took office, was to erect a monument dedicated to Houphouët Boigny, just to honor the man who paved the highway for him. Unfortunately no one gave him the right advice to do the right thing; the things that would trigger blessings upon a heir's life. Instead, he altered his course, and took the pathway to self-destruction.

Many of our African brothers don't realize that there is some kind of power in nature that gets activated when we do right by our elders. This is also a divine law.
So Bédié called upon himself a second curse by declining access to former First Lady: Therese Houphouët Boigny into the honor guests' room at the Airport. You don't have to be an anointed Prophet to know that Bédié was walking in the darkness, unable to identify the light that leads a lost man to a safe heaven.

As a matter of fact, his behavior proved that he was not in his right frame of mind to rule the country. While his supporters maintained that he was [the liberation hero] of the country, after he took over from the father, the rest of the Ivorian people including the militaries grew disenchanted. While many prayed for a change, the militaries were consulting to topple him.

The Ivorian people felt emptiness in the power. They were left on their own, fending for themselves like in a vessel without a captain. We were going to experience a coup d'état for the first time in the history of the country under President Bédié, as the manifestation of the curses he brought upon himself. He was so blindfolded and self-centered that nothing he did throughout his presidency made sense or did benefit the Ivorian people; except his entourage. Instead, poverty and misery became so blatant; tribalism and hatred were at a pick; conspicuously practiced as a culture. Bédié had no sound program to rule the country. The ship [Ivoire] was on the brink of capsizing. His entourage knew it, but they did nothing to call for rescue, or save it from drowning. Thus, Bédié's own behavior prompted his downfall.

At the aurora of his Presidency, President Bédié announced his [*ten projects*] consisting of his development program in a speech. When I asked his sympathizers in Washington DC to elaborate on the ten projects, none of them was able to do so accurately. So I asked one of my friends among them: "*Why is it so convoluted for you to comment on the program of your mentor?*
Why then are you following him?" Therefore, from what he did during that time, we identified a few items that perhaps constituted his ten projects:
1- He built two castles: one for his wife in her village, and
2- One in his own village. These two landmarks had night clubs in them, and the floors were covered with coins of 25, 50 and 100 Francs CFA.
3- A road that leads to his village from Abidjan deviating the city of Adzope,
4- An attraction park in Daoukro, his village,
5- A five stars hotel in Daoukro as well,
6-The creation of CNB as a substitute to PDCI, the father's party,
7-The application of the term *Ivoirité* that Alassane invented while serving as Prime Minister of the country,
8- A large government,
9- The imprisonment of journalists,
10- The creation of Bédié's own empire; preparing to consolidate another thirty years of dictatorship.
All these projects were not intended to benefit the Ivorian people. Throughout his presidency, Bédié created a high level of grief, and discontentment among the militaries, as well as the civilians. The

Ivorian people were praying for a change, as they had already come up to the conclusion that President Bédié was not the right man for the country. At one point, the militaries decided to launch a coup d'état, but when they consulted General Robert Gueï who was the Army's Chief of Staff at that time, to lead an insurgency to oust Bédié from power, he declined the offer. The same general Gueï was later fired by President Bédié on the ground of suspicion to plot a coup against him.
Sometimes when frightened, dogs bark at the wrong thing.

In 1995, during the preparation of the Presidential elections, Bédié managed to reject Alassane Ouattara's candidacy on the ground that he was not an Ivorian therefore ineligible in accordance with his new term "**Ivoirité**." In other words, Bédié is the father of the term "Ivoirité," that later became the center of all topics. Even though Bédié did not have the tools and the wits to properly manage this problem, he still invented it, and left it hanging. Furthermore, he created tribalism in the country on such a scale that husbands and wives who did not belong to the same tribe (Baoulé), or the same party (PDCI), divorced.
The most scandalous thing was that: many people lost their jobs simply because they did not militate in the PDCI.
Secret agents went around and lured people into conversations that were intended to determine their political inclination. From that point on they would either keep their jobs if they belonged to the PDCI party, or be dismissed without due process, if the agents proved that the person was a militant of FPI, President Gbagbo's party. He would then be banned from the premises. As a result of such practice fraught with hatred, unemployment rose to an unprecedented rate. In addition to that, we were also experiencing very weird and unusual circumstances in the country. Prices of commodities skyrocketed except in Daoukro, Bédié's hometown, where the same commodities were purchased at half price. This was difficult to explain. Only Bédié himself or his people could tell us what that meant. One morning people woke up and found that the price of a loaf of bread had doubled. A riot ensued, and for a week nobody knew were the president was, though he was in town.

Bédié was the most negligent Leader I have ever seen. He neither fought like many, nor suffered to be where he found himself, so he took this success for granted; otherwise, he would have acted with wisdom.

Time is essential, and very precious. When you still have it in your hand, it is wise to use it cleverly by acting right. Because when it runs out, there is no guarantee for a second chance; though everyone deserves one.

I see Bédié as the luckiest man on earth. Some people may see him as blessed because the opportunity he had, no other Ivorian has ever had it. And I may say that no other Ivorian will ever have it. Nevertheless, we need to admit this: Bédié messed up by making the wrong choices. Or should we say: with all the advisers he surrounded himself with; no one gave him the right advice?

As I mentioned earlier the freedom of choices in my foreword, we have to admit this: anybody could join the rebellion, or align with it with free will as we can see today, at the exception of one man in the country; Aimé Henry Konan Bédié. In Côte d'Ivoire, Bédié should be the only one to condemn it with all his energy, if no one else did, and stand firm on the side of the Republic. *Your father loved you; he made you king with the constitution of the country, not with guns. Therefore you should have been the only one to defend this constitution. You should be the one who sets the example of patriotism for his dignity. You have seen it all; from money to fame. You should not be competing against anyone and make up excuses why you did this or that. You should be seen today as a role model for the new generation.*

I want you to think about this:
Seven years have passed since the rebellion started. What have you achieved? You have wasted seven years in the lives of the Ivorian survivors. What would you have lost if you had let President Gbagbo do his first term peacefully, and have the election be organized afterwards?"

I find this difficult to understand that a person like Bédié can even be involved in the rebellion; after all these years at the side of Houphouët Boigny, and at the spotlight of the political life of the country. This is a shame. To me, the son of Houphouët should not be part of such dirty work.

A while later after the rebels failed, and made their stronghold in the North, one man who called himself Doh Felix went in the region of Zuenoula, and told the people that he came to defend the cause of General Robert Gueï. So he earned quick sympathy from the population. He deliberately ignited a conflict between the Wêh, and the Yacouba people. He recruited Liberian rebels who helped him burn villages of the Yacouba people in a very tricky way. He went in every village, asking the villagers to regroup for an emergency meeting on behalf of the slain General. When the people agreed and regrouped in one location, he suddenly came out, pretending to fetch a document in his vehicle. As he walked out of the house, and closed the door behind him, with the help of his Liberian recruits, they secured the door, and set the house at blaze. He did this in every location, and before the people could realize what was happening to them, it was too late. He had already burnt down a lot of villages, killing as many people as he could.

On his way to Liberia, he was killed by his own recruits. Probably he failed to honor the agreement he made with them. He downplayed the hazardous side of a breach of contract. When they searched him to recover their wages, they found documents revealing his true identity. His real name was N'dri Felix: native of Daoukro, former President Konan Bédié's hometown.

I discard the notion that former President Konan Bédié is unacquainted to N'dri Felix, and his crimes.

Bédié was involved in the destruction of the country he calls his own in many ways. He showed his fellow Ivorian his true identity and intentions. President Houphouët Boigny, the first President of the country, and his father bequeathed him a glorious legacy, leaving the destiny of the country in his hands. In return for lack of discernment, he messed it up. I hope that he learned from his many mistakes. But if he did not, then no need to bother. However if he can admit that he did, then I have an advice for him. I want to be reasonable and fair to personal everybody, because being an Ivorian fellow I have nothing against anyone. First, Bédié needs to apologize to the Ivorian people for his misconduct, his mistakes, and for leading the country to destruction, and for the lives of many he contributed in killing, creating desolation in many families.

Secondly, he needs to lay out a sound program that his followers will see and elaborate on, then set new goals and objectives that will pull the old party from the past, and update it to the exacting nature.

Thirdly, if he can not follow these above steps, I suggest that PDCI merely dismisses him, and finds a new leader.

To me, anybody can be a candidate to the Presidency as long as they fulfill the requirements. However, I exhort the senate to pass a law to instate "**a political debate**" for all the candidates. This will allow the Ivorian people to ask them questions during the campaign. I emphasize on that because people have taken advantage of the African populations for so long that, we can no longer tolerate negligent people coming to power and doing nothing for our countries and for our people.

For many years populations have been voting for candidates because they were related to them, or because they belonged to the same tribe, or religion; whether the person had an agenda or not, it did not matter to them. This nonsense has to stop, and constituents have to learn to vote for candidates' programs, instead of for who they are.

In conclusion to this chapter, here are the sponsors of the coup d'état against President Gbagbo, and the rebellion in Cote d'Ivoire: **President Jacques Chirac** of France, **Alassane Ouattara**, and former President of Côte d'Ivoire, **Henri Konan Bédié**.

Soro Guillaume was only recruited to lead the operation since he previously demonstrated the skills of shedding innocent blood at the University. He was the only qualified man for the job.

Chapter Four
UN and French Licorne troops in Côte d'Ivoire.
UN troops on sexual charges in DRC

QUITE NATURALLY, I thought that France, our erstwhile colonizer was trying to help an old colony, or a friend in need. I constantly mulled over the fact that Chirac was now trying to fix where he messed up previously by withholding military assistance to President Laurent Gbagbo on the basis of the non-existence of a military agreement between our two countries. So he ordered the UN and Licorne troops in [all honesty] to assist Côte d'Ivoire in resolving this crisis. No one would have ever imagined that the rebellion in Côte d'Ivoire was planned abroad in a glace Palace, by a person other than the people we had already in mind. Soro Guillaume the chief rebel was not the father of the rebellion. We were flabbergasted when we made the gruesome discovery.

At first, President GBAGBO refused the proposal for the deployment of UN and other troops in Côte d'Ivoire, but with the argument that these men were coming to help him disarm the rebels, and unify the country, he eventually gave in. Then he sought an answer to a key question: "Why UN and French troops at the same time, when we have the 43rd BIMA already stationed in the country?" He expressed his anguish over the deployment of the UN and French Licorne troops altogether.
"No, no, it is better to have two power structures stationed in Côte d'Ivoire because the problem that the country is facing is a serious matter," Chirac tried to pacify President Gbagbo.

When you are ill, why would you reject a doctor's willingness to prescribe you some medicine? You can never suspect him at first, or doubt whether he wants to poison you or not. All you want is to be healed; but in the long run when you feel that he is not acting right, you can dismiss him over negligence. "Let us assume that the troops are coming to help us get rid of the rebels, and attune our country." President Laurent Gbagbo said to himself, as 6000 UN and 4000 French Licorne started pouring in Côte d'Ivoire. From my stand point, the troops had a different, a special and a secret mission other than the one that was at stake in the country. Who would have thought that more that 10,000 troops would be deployed in Côte d'Ivoire, and stay for more that two years without accomplishing the mission we thought they came in for? And rather strive to keep the country divided?

Throughout the period of the various peace talks, we noticed that the rebels hit at numerous occasions, burning villages, and committing more crimes in full view of the Licorne and UN troops. We found these activities suspicious. Intelligence reported some ambiguous activities of the troops with the rebels.

For instance: according to an abstract from President Mamadou Koulibaly's book, co-written with Dr. Gary Bush, Professor at the University of Hawaii;

"The French army sent three Antonov-12 planes coming from Franceville, in Gabon. These planes registered as Ukrainian, were full of weapons in stock in Central Africa. The three planes took off from Durban, with military personnel and Ukrainian equipment. They landed in Liberia and in the rebels' stronghold in Côte d'Ivoire (Bouaké and Korhogo), where the weapons were delivered to the rebels."

Also, all the banks of Bouaké were vandalized by the rebels, under the supervision of the French troops.

Two years after the troops were deployed in Côte d'Ivoire, we saw no progress in terms of the disarmament of the rebels, and the unification of the country. Instead, more atrocities were reported in the West and Central West of the country where the troops were deployed.

In reality, the UN and other troops' time of stay in any country should be defined and limited, and the sender should make sure that they do not fail to accomplish whatever they were sent in for. I believe that Secretary General Kofi Annan did not send the UN troops in Côte d'Ivoire as an occupation force; but to accomplish a specific task, and then withdraw. Their mission, objectives, results to be reached, and the time needed to accomplish this mission should be made public. They should not stay beyond their time limit either, because: **First**, their mission is not to go and fight a war, but to settle the conflict and bring peace as quickly as possible.

Secondly, they have families to take care of in their respective places of residence.

Thirdly, they are human and they have needs; so the longer they stay, the more they are likely to engage in irrelevant businesses, and unethical affairs.

History has retained what these troops did in DRC. They were accused of raping and molesting young girls, and running a prostitution ring.

The Washington Post:

"An Investigation of UN on new cases of sexual abuse in DRC"
<u>Reuters</u> / Kinshasa, Congo, **August 17, 2006**.

"The UN is investigating a suspected child prostitution ring involving its peacekeepers and government soldiers in the Democratic Republic of Congo, the UN mission said on Thursday.

The UN declared in a letter that young vulnerable girls are lured to work as prostitutes by UN peacekeepers and government soldiers in the areas of South Kivu where they are deployed, a 17.000 member mission in Congo – the largest United Nations operation of peacekeeping in the world. The mission has been involved in a series of sexual scandals.

Earlier this year, a UN diplomat responsible for monitoring how the world body was tackling the problem, said sexual abuse charges against UN peacekeepers remained unacceptable high due to a persistent "culture of dismissiveness" in UN field missions. The UN mission declared that it is investigating the recent allegations on sexual abuse and insisted that there will be "zero tolerance" of the abuses of its troops.

"MONUC is taking these accusations very seriously and expressed a great shock to the testimonies of the victims of this illegal activity," said the organization.

As you can see, the risks factors are numerous. Prostitution becomes current as a result of poverty and war displaced victims. Since these men have currencies, they become an easy source of revenue for the desperate ones.

On the other hand, they become a subject for spreading diseases such as AIDS, and many STDs, if they are infected, or easy prays for those diseases in case they are healthy. Either way you look at it, it is not profitable for these troops to overstay in any country, nor advantageous for the population and the country in trouble.

I do not know the specifics of the contract of these troops in Côte d'Ivoire, but knowing that they came in because the country was in crisis, their mission could not be anything other than disarming the rebels, and restoring the integrity of the country. **Let us admit that whatever their assignment was**, they have failed as of **December 5th, 2005**. Therefore, they should depart without delay, because they are no longer needed by the Ivorian people.

Chapter Five
The veil falls off the face of Chirac (French President)
Patriotism in Côte d'Ivoire

IN THE MONTH OF OCTOBER 2004, the Government decided to eradicate the rebellion by launching an offensive called "Dignity." That was the right thing to do because rebellion is destructive. It is not something that people should pamper with, because: 1- rebellion is not meant to negotiate with, and 2- rebels have no feelings. On some occasions, they eat the flesh of their victims when they run out of food. Killing is a hobby to them, and human life has no value. So the plan of the Ivorian army was to destroy their cache of weapons, then follow up with a ground attack that would suppress the rebellion once for all. As intelligence was gathered, the Ivorian army hit precisely all the targeted points without missing a single one; thus destroying the rebels' total striking power.

At the ground attack, dumbfound, the Ivorian army (Fancy) experienced resistance, not from the rebels, but from the Licorne troops. The Ivorian army was eventually ordered to pull back from the offensive. So the brave and indefatigable soldiers withdrew very politely to defuse any foreseeable chaos that may have been pre-concerted by the French Licorne forces. By now we know how they operate: they are notorious for igniting confusion, blame the afflicted when they react, then use force in retaliation.

This offensive, even though court circuited, was a tremendous achievement in terms of debilitating the rebels. With the Licorne troops having stopped the Ivorian army, we did not rule out the true intentions of France and Chirac at this point. Then Chirac began to whine, claiming the death of 9 French soldiers, and an American Peace worker, and quickly, he mobilized the whole contingent of Licorne, as well as the marines of the 43rd BIMA base in Abidjan, Port Bouët. The death of the nine (9) French and the (1) American peace worker was an alibi to win the undivided support of America. Chirac realized he could not achieve what he was after on his own, so he sought help from the superpower on his trail to kill President Gbagbo. Especially when he heard words such as: "shoot at us; we are not afraid to die today, or tomorrow," from the young patriots, he got scared. And something in him told him:

"Look man; you have had your way for so long in the continent of Africa; but today, things have changed. It is going to be a different ball game from now on." So he decided to use the old trick that can easily make a man's blood boil. He was convinced that America would bite at his bait by hearing the death of its citizen. I praise the Lord for America for not paying attention to Chirac's lie. Why did the UN not investigate about the 9 French and the American worker that Chirac claimed died during the Ivorian army's offensive on the rebels' cache of weapons, and find out about the credibility of the information? Then if they were confirmed dead, determine the kind of business they were conducting with the rebels in their weapon storages at that time of the night. I have always asked myself: when did the presumed bodies leave Côte d'Ivoire to France and to the United States oblivious to the Ivorian people? If indeed they were killed, we would assume they died in the line of duty in a country at war.

Knowing that we would have never attacked deliberately the UN and French peacekeepers' positions, we would then apologize and pay them the due respect as heroes. We would then appoint some diplomats to represent our country at the funerals in Paris, as well as in the United States. This is what any intelligent mind would have expected to happen as opposed to what really took place. This attitude of Chirac stultifies the behavior of France in the eyes of the world.

I felt so embarrassed when a week later, I saw Chirac on TV at a funeral, standing tearfully by ten empty coffins of the nine French and one American who presumably died in Côte d'Ivoire, according to him.

Ironically; *since when was Chirac designated by the United States to burry American citizens who die abroad?*

America never held a funeral procession for an American citizen dying in Côte d'Ivoire during October or November 2004. No newspaper in the country published such news either. Anywhere in the world, no credible paper or Media organization ever published or even mentioned such news of the Ivorian army killing French or American civilians. The only Media sources that published such lies were French Medias; to back their President.

So to me, the real world knew the truth. But the French stuck to their guns, disregarding what the rest of the world would think about them. And subsequently, without considering other UN partners, the French troops began to destroy the Ivorian fighter planes that were sitting idle on the ground in Yamoussoukro.

Abstract from the archives of November 2004:
The French are assisting the rebels:

"Côte d'Ivoire has just been attacked by the French army. The traitors have destroyed our fighter Helicopters sitting idle on the ground in Yamoussoukro and Abidjan. They have also attacked the Guests' House of Yamoussoukro with heavy weapons, and they have killed many civilians by shooting at a crowd in Downtown Yamoussoukro.

After destroying our planes, the French soldiers have seized the international Airport Felix Houphouët Boigny in Abidjan, the Capital City. The Ivorian militaries have been subdued at their base of GATL. The French soldiers did not hesitate to shoot at the young bare handed patriots. A least five of them have died and many wounded. The French militaries are determined to slaughter the Ivorian people, and they have also besieged the two bridges that connect the City. They had snipers posted in the surrounding buildings, and have shot all night at the young patriots who were marching towards the Airport to protest the seizure of the Airport and the French occupation.

Col. Philippe Mangou (third from right), Commander-in-Chief of Côte d'Ivoire Army seen while inspecting wreckage of FACI Mi-8 helicopters destroyed by the French at the presidential residence in Yamoussoukro, on 7 November 2004. Immediately afterwards he ordered a pullback from offensive on rebels in the north.
(Photo: Emma)

Why such attitude of the French military marching on the city and killing the Ivorian people, when the local army only wanted to liberate their country that was under attack by assailants two years ago? The answer is simple. It was France that attacked Côte d'Ivoire in reality on September 19th, 2002. The rebels are only executing the order of their Master. As a matter of fact, the French Defense Minister Michelle Alliot Marie made it clear by saying: "President Chirac gave the order to the French soldiers to destroy the Ivorian fighter helicopters." But what she omitted to say was that: the French President Jacques Chirac has by the same occasion ordered the soldiers to shoot at anything that moves. The repression was bloody. And the soldiers of the fifth military power in the world did not hesitate to shoot at the young patriot boys and girls with naked hands who were only angry at the betrayal of France to their country. This is a country (France) that is known to be the promoter of democracy and human rights. This is a country that can not balance its budget without the resources of Côte d'Ivoire. While France is mistreating the Ivorian population, her citizens are living in such an insulting opulence at the bank of the Ebrié Lagoon.
In conclusion: betrayal, cupidity, selfishness are the appropriate words among many that characterize this France of Chirac.
This France of Chirac has just betrayed Côte d'Ivoire by slaughtering the innocuous Ivorian people, and jeopardizing a precious friendship of many years that is profitable to her.

The Ivorian army defeated the rebels on all the front lines, but soon will lose the positions recaptured from the hands of the rebels because of France that is

repositioning the rebels. Côte d'Ivoire will still be divided in two, while France is arming back the rebels. And Soro Guillaume and his killers will resume talking, insulting and threatening. France is planning to impose a Prime Minister of consensus to the Ivorian people, with ministers who can not even write their names. And worst, the same France is envisioning installing at the head of our country, a President of his choice, as if we were back to the era of the colonization of Africa. But this France of Chirac that is killing the Ivorian children to impose his rules to an independent country for forty years needs to know that it is not finished. There is an equation which Chirac did not probably think of; that equation is "the Ivorian people" who love their President, is united and determined to thwart neo-colonization. This population that walked all night to defend the values it believes in is not ready to back down before France and her assassins. Vietnam won the war with bamboos. Algeria did the same with faith. France can kill as many children, she will not impose us her will in spite of all the strategies she is devising. Dramane Ouattara is now working on his inaugural speech as President of Côte d'Ivoire in the capital city of Gabon. He needs to stop day dreaming, in spite of the malevolent advices he is receiving from the short man of Libreville, who thinks that he has power over the Ivorian politics."
Author, **Franck DALLY**

After treading on Yamoussoukro, the French militaries proceeded in direction of Abidjan with tens of mortars and war vehicles. This unrelenting behavior gave an alarming signal out to the Ivorian patriots. Their movement towards Abidjan was seen as suspicious, so the patriots came out, and stood along the way to see what they were up to. As they entered Abidjan, the Capital City of Côte d'Ivoire, they took the direction of Cocody, the dwelling place of President Laurent Gbagbo. When the Ivorian official asked them where they were going, they responded that they had lost their way. In the meantime, Helicopters hovered above. The young patriots then took to the streets and followed them to impede their proceeding. The contingent was forced to stop at the Hotel Ivoire, and the patriots stood by the thousands between them and the President's Residence, adjacent to the prestigious Hotel Ivoire where French snipers were already posted awaiting for Chirac's signal. The tension was high that day on both the Ivorian and French sides.

The French soldiers' attitude was very provocative, but what I personally admired was the balmy attitude of the Ivorian army. The whole country came to a point of stand still for a while as the army generals of both sides were interacting. Although we had a vague idea of a probable mission against our President, we did not know for sure what it entailed, until we heard the detail plan of action from the French Defense Minister, Mrs. Michelle Alliot Marie:

"Laurent *Gbagbo is going to pay for this the hard way*," she said on public television. From this point, it was all clear that Chirac was after President Laurent Gbagbo. The plan was to kill him or abduct him. Eventually, Chirac's plan of deposing President Gbagbo was foiled by the angry and stern patriots, even though unarmed. They gave their chests to protect their country and their President, and no circumstances of any nature would be bombastic enough to deter them. The French troops on the other hand were not willing to retract. The pilot of the helicopter received the signal to shoot at the President's residence, but something weird unfolded.

"I don't see the residence; all I see is a bush," the pilot said on his radio when he was given the signal to shoot.

"You are right above it; shoot," the order came back to him.

"I don't know what you are talking about; I am flying above a swampy bush. I even see some Buffalos running ahead of me. Do you want me to shoot at them? " the pilot responded to the command center. This event went on for hours, but the pilot of the helicopter could not see the President's residence and shoot. The unsuccessful accomplishment of that mission rattled Chirac and his defense Minister's nerves, so they gave order to the snipers posted on the 12th floor of the hotel Ivoire to shoot randomly at the patriots in order to scare them away. So they began to spray them with bullets. Unfortunately, the bullets did not solve the problem.

Many French citizens living in Abidjan or in the country were outraged by the atypical behavior of the French marines, and the devastated consequences of their brutality. At the same time, they feared for their own lives, so they called their Ambassador and requested to be airlifted for protection. They knew that such provocative behavior could easily escalate into an incontrollable act of retaliation. They knew that the Ivorian youths were very angry; and so irritated that there was a possibility that they might lash at any French national in the country as a result of this. Eventually it did happen that day as a human reaction. Fortunately, beside the material damage, no lives of French citizen were claimed.

All human on earth have a violent side inside him that sleeps like a dormant volcano. This side will never show if all human (black and white, yellow and green) were to cultivate mutual respect and consideration at all time, regardless of the color of the skin. Sadly though, the French have no consideration for the black man.

They think they have the right to destroy the black men's properties when they feel like it. They can spray bullets on their children as they wish, and then sanction them on top of their wounds and dead children, and get away with that.

France's behavior in Côte d'Ivoire:

1- France's behavior in Côte d'Ivoire in November 2004 confirms that she had an important role in the planning of the foiled coup d'état. Also this tells us that she is the cause of most conflicts, rebellions, civil wars, and genocides in French-Africa.

2- The behavior of our neighbors in this crisis reveals that they were involved, many contributed, or at least were aware of the foiled coup d'état against President Laurent Gbagbo. **3-** The behavior of our Ivorian brothers in the opposition depicts that they organized themselves to prevent President Gbagbo from governing. As proof, they are holding on tight to the rebels in one hand, and in the other they are talking about peace process. The reality is that, they are looking for a crack in the wall to penetrate. Make no mistake about it; if they find an opportunity, they will take advantage of it.

Notice this:

Rebellion is not formed to negotiate with its target. Rebellion is not a friendly entity that pledges negotiations. It is always launched against a regime, a government, an individual (a President), who rebuffs the colonial rules. Rebellion comes to clean up, and make way for the installation of someone else favorable to the colonizers.

Therefore, the local rebels have only one mission: terrorize (kill, steal, and destroy.) Their goal is to overthrow the actual President, and seize the State run Media.

Also, no one takes weapons today, and disarms the next day on request. So do not expect the rebels in Côte d'Ivoire to disarm anytime soon; nevertheless, we hope they do.

In November 2004, it became all plausible that the real rebel who attacked us during the night of **September 19th 2002**, in the attempt to overthrow President Laurent Gbagbo, was no one else other than **Jacques Chirac;** President of France, from **May 17th 1995 to May 17th 2007.**

Chirac's parents lived in Côte d'Ivoire before the independence year, in a village called Abotro; in the region of Guitry, in the County of Divo. They owned lands, and had plantations there. During that time, information reveals that they had a child; (a baby boy) in the year 1932.

Curiously, according to French Register's Office, Chirac was born in the 16th District of Paris, in the year 1932. How strange and ambiguous this is, to have one's parents living in Côte d'Ivoire and having a child there in 1932, and be born in Paris from the same parents, that same year?

From this, I understand how humiliating it would be for the President of France to be born in Africa, in a village. So altering the information in the attempt to erase all links with the black continent, and then building a total white image in compliance with his eligibility, can easily be overlooked. This falsification of the records could be viewed as a fraudulent act if it was the other way around. A racist can never accept to be biologically linked to a black country. When Chirac grew up, he regularly came to visit President Houphouët Boigny in Côte d'Ivoire. It was during one of his visits that a palm reader revealed his future Presidency in France.

Chirac had such a tremendous opportunity for being linked to Côte d'Ivoire, and connected to the continent of Africa. First, he could claim the Ivorian nationality anytime, and perhaps one day, decide to retire in Côte d'Ivoire after serving as President of France. Legally, no jurisdiction would deny him this right, if proven so. Unfortunately he has blown it out by double-crossing the Ivorian people.

His two terms as President of France were a disaster, shaped by improprieties that have dealt a perennial fissure on the dignity of the former great nation of France. The French people were so desperate for a leader that they did not consider impeaching him after he literally disintegrated the image of the country.

Secondly, the African leaders could be his best friends knowing that Africa has so many resources that would benefit France in the long terms. Instead, France's foreign politics in Africa under Chirac has been so contumelious that, anyone on earth would think that France does not need Africa at all. Chirac dealt personally with Côte d'Ivoire so contemptuously over the past seven years, from 2002 until he left office in 2007, that now, the relationship between the two countries has taken a sharp blow. He chose intimidation and weapons instead of diplomacy to interact with Côte d'Ivoire on one hand, and the African countries on the other. He is about to learn grimly that there is one Power above all powers; the Power of God; which is the Ivorian people's cornerstone. Also the power of nature is more powerful than the power of the mortars and the Kalashnikovs he is relying on.

Nature will never allow anyone to destroy the land that witnessed their birth. As Chirac decided to destroy Côte d'Ivoire, at that point if one does not get earlier advice to repent and ask forgiveness and burn his guns, the power of nature can reverse the equation, and turn it into reflexivity, and self-destructive type of mechanism. Human does not have enough to give back what is due to nature, and the land of birth. Patriotism to me is essential to show love to the land of your birth, because no one teaches patriotism; it comes from within. Once you express it as a human, you automatically enter into the fullness of the creator and most

High, God Almighty. We can prove this by looking around us.

Nature around us is constantly evolving and the evolution of plants and animals in the nature is occurring in a matter of days and weeks in some instances.

The green world around us is a scene of constant, sophisticated chemical warfare, with plants producing pesticides in response to attacks, and insects developing resistance. When human develop resistance to protect their country, their people, and their sovereignty against predators, some of us who call themselves the heirs of President Houphouët Boigny, (the Houphouëtists) are outraged. You can tell they have no clue about patriotism.

They ignore what it means. This is one of the major reasons why the continent of Africa is still a third world continent. Some African leaders did not demonstrate any regard, and sold the landmarks of resources of their countries to the highest bidder for 100 years or so to be exploited, and got rich out of those deals. We have cases of countries that export oil, Gold, and Diamond, and still the populations live in abject poverty.

Côte d'Ivoire was certainly in that predicament until President Gbagbo came into power on October 31st, 2000, and initiated his re-foundation program. A true patriot would never see his country in that condition and not take any action. As soon as he questioned the existence of the colonial taxes payable to France in accordance with the colonial contracts, he became a target. That is the reason why Chirac decided to topple him by launching the coup d'état against him.

This is the real cause of the attack of September 19th 2002, and all the mischief that continue to spatter today.

At this point, here are the sponsors of the genocide, and the masterminds behind the coup d'état and the rebellion against President Gbagbo: **1- Alassane Dramane Ouattara, 2- Jacques Chirac,** then President of France, and **3- Henri Konan Bédié,** former President of Côte d'Ivoire.

Patriotism in Côte d'Ivoire:

Chapter Six
The destabilization of Côte d'Ivoire

CÔTE D'IVOIRE WAS THE MOST PRESTIGIOUS country in the region of South Sahara between the years 1965 and 1985. It was noted for its economical and political stability. As the world leader of cocoa and coffee production, it became a place of interest and attraction, thus luring a stream of immigrants from neighboring countries. A small country of 322,000 square miles, and a population ranging now between 14 and 18 million inhabitants, was seen as the promise land for all the foreigners who poured in, even before the 60's. The Ivorian people were happy with all the foreigners who eventually enjoyed living in Côte d'Ivoire. They were of a tremendous help in the agricultural sector of our economy. For decades foreigners were considered as brothers and sisters to the Ivorian people.

Peace was presumed as the speech of former President Felix Houphouët Boigny kept the Ivorian people in a state of slumbers. He preached peace and self- sufficiency while the majority of the Ivorian population was living in an illusion of prosperity. The Ivorian people were being fooled by the propaganda of this illusionary wealth, while they were chocking with the mixture of agony and respect for the father and President, Houphouët Boigny. No one dared raise his finger in the country, to scream, and denounce the imminent danger that haunted Côte d'Ivoire. The Ivorian nationals were held in abject poverty, struggling daily to keep up with the skyrocket prices of commodities, and life's vicissitudes.

All that time, the Ivorian people did not know that they were being taken hostage by their immediate and remote neighbors who had poured in over the years, and now represented a high percentage of the total population. They were living in an era of two extreme tendencies, where a sudden class of extremely rich men was growing in a desert of dry bones. The ordinary Ivorian man lived jobless or penniless with a job, and farmers with their families hungered, dying sometimes from a minor migraine or fever. Things that people take for granted in developed countries had become a myth. Little by little the middle class vanished, and things grew dramatically out of control. Only politicians and foreigners were making two ends meet. The weird thing about it was that foreigners came in with nothing, but after little over two years, they were business owners. The Ivorian banks were practicing the culture of lending to foreigners without collateral in order to establish any business of their choice. All an ordinary Ivorian man was entitled to in a local bank was his pay, his deposit, or an advance on pay day. If he worked, he would get the equivalent of his account balance, or twice or four times his monthly salary as a loan. The few who made the exception by overriding the banks' culture were sponsored by relatives in high government positions. Besides those, the majority of them were living in a haze, feeding on the nicely written speeches of the Ministers who were outlining promises of Castles in Spain.

I literally saw a population kept in a dream world, unable to question or complain about all these promises that were made a decade or more ago, and were never kept.
For example one Minister, now I can't recall who, announced the construction of a Metro rail system in the 1970's. Twenty three years later, even before President Houphouët Boigny died, people never mentioned it even in a simple conversation as if it was never promised. I am citing just this example among myriad frivolous promises. We lived in an era of more words with no actions. This

doesn't mean that we lacked the resources to build those infrastructures. That was the time of the economic boom of Côte d'Ivoire, and the country was counted among the most stables in the continent. We could undertake any type of investment if we wanted. Sadly, more money was squandered on unnecessary things rather than investing in housing, public transportation, education, employment, social services, and many more in anticipation of bad times.

Between the year 1980 and 1993, before he died, the father was so stricken with age that he was unable to follow up with every piece of paper presented to him for his signature. *He might have signed for his own resignation or death unknowingly*. His entourage took advantage of his state of mental deficiency to play with him. They engaged in embezzlement, and pumped huge sums of money into peripheral banks overseas. No wonder why we have extremely rich people in Côte d'Ivoire today than anywhere else in the continent. For example, the government workers who died over the years were still having their pay checks printed. Anybody with a straight mind would have assumed that the purpose for printing these checks was to support their families and orphans. Obviously, no one would have believed otherwise. These crooks in suit and ties only cared for themselves and what they could get from the country's safes. No wonder why today they have no clue about the expression of patriotism, and they call the patriots: "Laurent Gbagbo's militia."

One thing very noticeable in the country was that we were at peace, presumably, simply because as time went by, all the scavengers were unobtrusively stealing, draining and siphoning the country's money, while others were remotely feeding on the relic of our economy. What made things worse was the fact that none of these people feared the law and the justice system in the country. As long as the country was ran in such a snarling condition, and things were kept that way, unchanged, with the same kind of speech and practices, the Ivorian people would be at peace forever, while dying slowly within. And any person, who would come up with attempt to change things in ways that would constitute hindrance to thefts and embezzlements, would obviously be treated as [**the bad guy**].

Throughout that time, the country was geared in a jungle like direction where nothing was controlled and managed properly. Corruption, theft, and illicit enrichment were practiced conspicuously. This chaotic type of leadership is obviously what the colonizers encourage because they benefit from it.

President Houphouët Boigny had managed to secure his empire for life by institutionalizing the one party system. He had progressively instilled fear in the minds of the population about multi-party system since the massacre of the Guébié people. No one wanted to suffer such atrocities again, and Houphouët himself could not afford bloodshed of the sort any more; so now the only option that was left to the estranged population was his death, although no one wished for it. Until then no one would dare complain or think of any kind of change. Suggesting a Multi Party System would mean [a sacrilege] to him.

Therefore, the unsympathetic, yet starving population found itself alienated, praying quietly for a messiah to come to the rescue one day.

IN 1986, ONE MAN, AND ANOTHER SON of Gagnoa risked not only his own life, but the lives of the Bété people as he launched another political party to challenge the PDCI. *The possibility of a second massacre on the same ethnic group was lurking.*

The emergence of Koudou Laurent Gbagbo into politics appeared as the return of Kragbé Gnagbé, and it was likely to produce another slaughter, after the cruelties inflicted on the Guébié people; a sub-group of the Bété tribe, in 1970. Kragbé Gnagbé died along with his people for initiating multiparty system in Côte d'Ivoire at a time when former President Houphouët Boigny was still shaping his empire. The cause was just, but Kragbé found himself at the wrong place at the wrong time, like Ernest Boka who died in prison for similar reasons. This rising tide whetted Houphouët Boigny's hatred for the Bété ethnic group, because of Kragbé Gnagbé, as well as the Abe tribe because of Ernest Boka. Now, here came Laurent Gbagbo a few years later to add up to Houphouët Boigny's resentment and bitterness against the two above mentioned tribes.

Personally Houphouët Boigny could not afford another massacre on his people, so he eventually gave in after numerous attempts to thwart the new threat failed. He reluctantly favored the multiparty system; thus the first official opposition party named the FPI: (the Ivorian Popular Front,) was founded. Koudou Laurent Gbagbo, one of the founding members was appointed Secretary General. He literally challenged Houphouët Boigny, even pushed him to retire prematurely at one point. In 1990, for the first time the Ivorian people experienced a Presidential Election with two candidates to choose from. Visibly, Laurent Gbagbo became the messiah for whom the Ivorian people prayed quietly, asking God to send them a redeemer. His persistence made the old man realized that it was time for change. However, he refused to let go. In spite of his age, Houphouët Boigny still held on tight as if he was afraid the population might discover his mistakes. Eventually, as no human is the master of time and circumstances, his resistance eventually gave way. Laurent Gbagbo's emergence was seen as a breakthrough for the Ivorian people. On the other hand, he was perceived from distance by the colonial despots as a threat to their interests and by the local politicians as a beast trying to meddle with their culture. They were certainly outraged because after so many years of practice of what had become a chronic syndrome of embezzlement and siphoning of public funds, it wouldn't be easy for them to survive just on a salary as the rest of the Ivorian people.

President Laurent Gbagbo, formerly general secretary of his party, the (FPI), came with a counter speech that seethed the tenants of the house.

"Côte d'Ivoire can be governed differently. If the wealth of this country is managed wisely and allocated appropriately, every citizen of this country can have three meals a day. We can even provide free Medicare for every child and every mother, and medical insurance for every farmer," Laurent Gbagbo asserted in his overture address to the nation. This kind of speech was viewed as abominable by those who would become his opponents a decade later. From that point on, the politicians of the old system began to devise plans in order to kill his ideas before they could ever take form in the future. Not to mention that the colon Chirac who knew that France fed on dubious, and crooked contracts that were written before the independence of the African countries, was already on the look out. He knew that France could not survive without these ominous deals. On the same token, he knew well that no change could ever be effective in any French colony in Africa with these colonial contracts still in effect.

THE TRUTH OF THE MATTER IS THAT the progress of Africa is repelled by the colonial burdens weighing over the African countries; therefore these colonial contracts constitute the drawback for the development of Africa. And Chirac and others knew for sure that one day, sooner or later there would be a new breed of Leaders like President Laurent Gbagbo, who would start to spout the nonsense that is keeping us back. He knew for a fact that concerning Côte d'Ivoire, [**the protected Treasure Land**] of France, President Gbagbo would target those colonial contracts as soon as he takes office; so Chirac begun to be at odd with him. If he could stop him from coming to power at once, he would. Unfortunately, he did not have that kind of repressive magic. So when President Laurent Gbagbo was later elected, and sworn in as the new President of Côte d'Ivoire in October 2000, it was already planned that Chirac and the Ivorian opposition would join forces in order to prevent their brother from ruling. The Ivorian politicians knew that President Laurent Gbagbo was politically advanced; so allowing him to rule was considered a fatal mistake they could not afford. In addition, they knew he had a sound program for the country; and allowing him to implement it would be considered disastrous. Therefore, the only option left to them in terms of having something to lean on and speculate was to create a state of chaos and confusion in the country, then point the finger at him. Other than that, they had the gut feeling that if nothing was done to hinder any normal course of action, in the long run, they would be exposed by their political rival and the estranged population would discover their selfish ways and apathetic behaviors, and eventually disown them. They were conscious of that, so they strived to prevent it.

As we can see throughout this crisis, they have successfully reached the disconcerting condition they planned to create by disrupting President Gbagbo's first term. A multitude got killed in the process. Many villages disappeared, and the country was partitioned, and maintained in that brittle state by the French troops under the cover of UN Peacekeepers. What we are grateful of is that so far, they have not been able to take control as planned, as much as they tried.

The panoramic range of the crisis suggested that:

- Chirac certainly agreed to provide the weapons, and the international and political pressure needed.
- Alassane Ouattara agreed to take care of the payroll of the rebels.
- Bédié and Banny served as backbones, to provide the logistics, and extra funding for the project. All the Banks of Bouaké were vandalized, and the head of the prominent financial institution said nothing. The Ivorian opposition would keep the harassment on going while the killings were done by the rebels.
- Our neighbors agreed to give their soil for the training of the rebels, and for their weapon storage.
- The entire region was aware of this plan of destabilization of our country; no question about that.

According to the planning, the logistics and the means used to implement this attack, the assailants were sure to quickly get things under control. The sponsors and the organizers were also sure to shift the leadership of the country the following day. Alassane Dramane Ouattara was probably day-dreaming; seeing himself as the future President of Côte d'Ivoire in a matter of hours. He was probably seeping Champagne in a waiting confinement, or perhaps rehearsing his inaugural speech. At one point during the unrest of November 2004, Alassane hid in one of the French mortars, waiting for Chirac to kidnap President Gbagbo, to install him as the new President of Côte d'Ivoire, in the midst of such an overbearing chaos. What an audacity? He is truly a [**Brave Tchê**.] Unfortunately, they never expected an adverse output; failure was never an option.

Because they have failed to overthrow President Laurent Gbagbo, the enemies of Côte d'Ivoire have only one word in their mouths just to cover up their embarrassment: **"Laurent Gbagbo is the obstacle of the peace process. He has to leave office,"** without defining the type of obstacle he is, and the reasons why they are all against him. Neither the rebels, nor the politicians, no one says with convincing arguments what it is that they are reproving of him.

As they failed to physically remove him from power, for five years they have put pressure on President Laurent Gbagbo through numerous resolutions, meetings, and senseless accords with Chirac at the command. Clearly, actions of France to promote rebellions, civil wars, and genocides in Africa have nowhere been so flagrant and deliberate than in Côte d'Ivoire. He probably thought he was permitted to do anything as if he was the owner of Côte d'Ivoire. Secretary General Kofi Annan of the U.N openly joined President Jacques Chirac in fomenting a constitutional coup d'état aimed at taking away the executive powers of the democratically elected President of Côte d'Ivoire, President Laurent Gbagbo.
The whole picture of the scenario depicted that all our neighbors and friends; the African Union, and the ECOWAS, knew about what was going to take place in Côte d'Ivoire, and all of them

seemingly favored it.   At the most thorniest point of the crisis, the whole world saw a devoted and indefatigable President, determined to collect the broken pieces to put his country back together. As he struggled and gave his best through the entire period of the crisis, his enemies followed him and scrutinized every action he took, and every step he made. They then translated them perversely to their advantage, and accused him of anything. That is why in spite of all the sacrifices and efforts he made throughout the time of the crisis, he was always viewed as the guilty party. In some instances he made decisions knowing that they were wrong, but for the sake of bringing peace back in his country and to deaden the sufferings of the Ivorian people, he made them. For instance he agreed to bring the rebels in the government knowing that it was a wrong think naturally. But for the sake of peace, he signed the decree, thinking that it would help. Surely, the rebels joined the first government of transition with the sole aim to get close to him as an enemy, not for the development of the country. In the end this did not work, so the rebels went back and resumed the killing.

At one point I even described the President's actions as an innocent man sharing a room with a snake unknowingly. He granted most of the rebels' requests; but the more he gave out, the more he was pushed the back against the wall. The whole opposition in Côte d'Ivoire and some neighboring Presidents were visibly rallying against him. On the other hand, Chirac began to openly attack him verbally after his plan with Kofi Annan of the U.N, and the entire Ivorian opposition failed. Looking at the whole picture, you could see that the whole world was against Côte d'Ivoire. No other country would have survived this; but Côte d'Ivoire did because the Lord of Host was with us. He led President Laurent Gbagbo through the war, even with an under-equipped army. The Lord fought for us and pushed the assailants back to the Northern part of the country, as he did for the children of Israel during the Biblical era.

Ever since Laurent Gbagbo chose to do politic, even when

he contended Houphouët Boigny and he couldn't win the election, the idea of toppling Houphouët never crossed his mind. Instead he pursued his dream, and he continued to educate the Ivorian people on the real issues to which the country was confronted. President Houphouët Boigny knew that he was dealing with a determined, stern, and intelligent fellow who, not only loves his country, but who knew what he wanted. From this point on, the message became clear in Houphouët Boigny's mind that it was time to go.

As much as he wanted to be President of Côte d'Ivoire, Laurent Gbagbo never forced the issue. He knew that the right season would come. Many people pushed him to seek the shortcut to the Presidency, but he always turned down such consideration: "I know what you are asking me, but this is not the philosophy of our party. We will be in power one day through election," he always answered. Throughout his period of opposition, we never experienced a single coup d'état in Côte d'Ivoire. Now that he is in office, the Ivorian politicians of the opposition have formed partnership with France to organize coup d'états. They have formed various alliances and have devoted all their efforts for the destabilization of their own country, Côte d'Ivoire, just to get rid of their brother.

Our neighbors played a significant role in the destabilization of our country as well. This practice shows how selfish, wicked, and self-centered some of our leaders are. This behavior depicts the familiar cycle of penance established between the colonizers and their dictator satraps in Africa; a vicious circle of sycophants who have done nothing else but to serve as purveyors of the continent's resources, and steal our countries blind. For instance, there are tales of countries so small in the continent of Africa; with a total population not exceeding two million inhabitants that are huge oil exporters, and that are experiencing appalling difficulties in terms of creating opportunities for the growing generations. And you wonder where all this money from the oil revenues goes? A country so small with these revenues, the government could allocate $5000.00 to each family a year if nothing else was done, and not feel a thing. Unfortunately, these resources are meant to pay the colonial overheads, and the remaining is divided among the Government officials, leaving the populations starving. You can see that these dictators have purposely led such a rich continent astray, smearing its image and turning it into a worthless land, and a dumping ground for toxic wastes coming from the West; **WHAT A SHAME**?

The Courier of Abidjan – 11/21/2005 10:39:37 PM.
"Jeune Afrique the Intelligent" (JAI), # 2341 of November 20- 25, 2005, in the "Confidential" column.

"For his movements in Europe, and namely in France where resides his family, Guillaume Soro uses most of the time the diplomatic passport that the Senegalese authorities gave him: as opposed to his Ivorian passport which does not allow him to obtain a visa," says our friend from **Jeune Afrique the Intelligent,** *who mentions that "this favor from Wade and his administration to Soro, is somehow appreciable knowing that the French consulate authorities do not deliver visas to any Ivorian nationals."*

This diplomatic passport from the Senegalese authorities, according to JAI, allows Guillaume Soro to easily connect African, as well as French and European capitals; such as Dakar, Accra, Abuja, Libreville, Ouagadougou, Paris and Bonn..." With such favor from Wade, the chief rebel can boast and live like a king."

In Paris, according to JAI, Soro always resides in a hotel located in the 16th district. Under the cover of Chirac, he is exempt from all restrictions, in spite of his inflammatory language, and the violations of human rights committed in the Northern region that he occupies illegally. His wages as Minister of communication (more than 5 millions francs CFA per month=$12000.00) and his revenue as chief of rebellion, reveals JAI, allow him to rent in Franksville, a Parisian suburb, an apartment for his family and more so, to sustain his many expenses. Because of the support from African heads of states; Wade, Blaise Compaoré, ATT... and the colon Chirac, disregarding the accord of non assault included in the chart of the ECOWAS, Guillaume Soro can be free to make fun of the legal Ivorian authorities." (**Saint-Claver Oula, Author**.)

Former President Diouf contradicts President Wade's thesis.

According to press release from **Agence France Presse** (AFP), the former Senegalese Head of State declared yesterday on a French public Radio Station, RFI that:

"President Gbagbo, with all his supporters should consider revising the article 35 by the National Assembly and immediately after, the whole International Community will be mobilized for the second objective: the disarmament, the re-unification of the country, a referendum for the approbation of the Constitution and the elections."

This intervention from Mr. Diouf came after the one from his successor who affirmed a few days ago that the elections needed to be postponed, and rather form "an independent technocratic government of the opposition parties that will be in charge of leading a transition of four to five years." President Diouf's proposition, even though does not take into account the provisions of the Ivorian Constitution can not see the beginning of a modification as long as the country is partitioned, but deserves to be more serious and can constitute a basis of discussion among serious men. Unlike the nonsense declared these days by Wade, who is giving the impression to want to sabotage the South African mediation conducted by President Thabo M'beki. In fact, we recall the same Wade who at the beginning of the crisis, shot President Eyadema in the legs as he was two steps away from concluding a peace deal between the parties. Wade's malicious acts allowed France to interfere directly in the conflict to implement the round table of Marcoussis.

Author; Guillaume T. Gbato

What is it about Côte d'Ivoire that our neighbors are going crazy wanting to destabilize it by all means necessary? And they even ignore their own problems and issues in their own countries.

Washington Express Newspaper, reports on 10/19/2006

<u>Thiaroye</u>, Senegal

" At a funeral in this Senegalese fishing town, mothers wept for their sons - dozens of whom drowned when the wooden craft they hoped to take to Europe was caught in a storm.

The group from that March funeral has grown to 357 women – all having lost a son, husband or cousin who set out on a perilous voyage hoping for a better life. A Canary official said that more than 500 bodies have been recovered in the waters between Africa and Europe.

Many would-be migrants and their relatives argue that the journey is the only option they have to improve their lives, when jobs at home are scarce – and the traditional work in fishing and agriculture don't easily support large families," said Mr. Fall.

Heidi Vogt, (AP) Author.

Why take the opportunities away from these young men and women, and redirect them to rebels for the destabilization of neighboring countries? Wade, a former opposition leader who spoke the truth once; what has gone wrong with him to want to destabilize Côte d'Ivoire, when he has crucial issues to deal with at home? It is clear that many African leaders' priority is to please the colon over the life of their citizens, and their countries. The wellbeing of their fellow citizens comes last if it matters at all. If it did, people like Wade would not center their energy on destabilizing neighboring countries. He would have taken measures instead to prevent the massive death toll of young Senegalese seeking opportunities in Europe, at sea.

I understand why Chirac always says he knows the psychology of the people of West Africa. He knows that many are traitors, senselessly and purposely betraying their own continent by welcoming rebellion for the destruction of their own, as well as neighboring countries. Wade might as well send an Ambassador to the rebels held territory so he could better cooperate with Soro Guillaume, and continue to be a provider for the rebels. I wonder if Wade cares about the lives of his citizens who live in Côte d'Ivoire. Or does he think that when Soro and his killers snap and resume their killing spree, they will spare only the Senegalese in the country. As if they ask their victims to show proof of nationality before shooting them. Today, the rebels are treated as heroes by our neighbors; people we have called our friends all these years. This is unbelievable. We did not know that we were surrounded by our enemies all this time. This behavior of our friends and neighbors confirms that history repeats itself. In the Old Testament, the children of Israel were surrounded by the Amelikites, the Pharisees, the Philistines and many more. They fought against them all in order to conquer the promise land.

Today, here we are in the New Testament, surrounded by a legion, people we call neighbors or aligning countries, who, by their actions can be sworn as enemies today. They attacked us by night, and failed to overthrow the government of President Laurent Gbagbo. They have used their myriad back up plans and have also failed, because JESUS CHRIST reassures us that: **"they will wage war against you, but they will never prevail**- because **He** who leaves in us is mightier and greater than he who comes against us."

GOD HAS USED THIS CRISIS TO REVEAL, AND EXPOSE ALL THE ENEMIES OF CÔTE D'IVOIRE.

Chapter Seven
UN's implication in the crisis of Côte d'Ivoire

THE (UN) UNITED NATIONS; IS THE MOST PROMINENT human organization that exists on the face of the earth; consequently, it is prone to be the most respected human organization.

The UN should be more involved in actions such as preventing crisis from happening in countries, and drafting effective agendas on the ground levels of those countries whenever troops are deployed and sent in. But the intervention process in which the UN is engaged, and the writing of sanctions it specializes in are all incongruous with the rank it occupies in the world of the living. Eventually, the UN should never venture in writing sanctions on demand - like what took place between Jacques Chirac, (now former President) of France, and Côte d'Ivoire in November 2004.

The UN may sanction a country after several warnings. And in the end when that country refuses to cooperate, rebuffing the UN's recommendations regarding the matter, then a sanction can be sought. Otherwise, there is no ground for sanctions especially if such country had not previously had any kind of misunderstanding; needless to mention a conflict, with the organization.

Why would the UN's Security Council not study all the facts carefully before making the decision to sanction a country that is a member of the organization, when one country requests a sanction against another? Unless it is clarified that there are first class, and third class members, at the UN. Why would the UN, (**an organization that was created to promote justice**), practice the Rule of the jungle? I am not blaming the organization; because I believe that this atypical conception and law-breaking theory are the fruits of the morality of the [overseer] of its business at that time. I am more than certain that the UN has an internal structure, among which is an investigation body. If such is the case, why then would the Security Council base [its decision making process] on the feelings, and emotions of an individual? In this case, people should be sincere, and straightforward with the African people, and tell them that:

"Because Africa was colonized by France, and others, it is classified as a subordinate continent, therefore has no right to the common justice that all people deserve."

This would help us understand our fate, and not complain, knowing our history.

The UN's sanction of weapon ban against Côte d'Ivoire in November 2004 was dictated by Jacques Chirac to the Secretary General Kofi Annan, who granted it hastily to please him. This weapon ban was discriminatory and blasphemous because it did not include the rebels. I am sure Kofi Annan heard about the first attack on Côte d'Ivoire done by Soro and his killers, **on September 19th 2002**; and the second attack by the French Marines of the Licorne in **November 2004**. And the Secretary General of the UN made no comment whatsoever to condemn these acts, nor investigated that matter to find out whether Chirac's alibi concerning the nine French, and the American he claimed were killed, was credible. He implicitly approved of these attacks. But, when Jacques Chirac asked him to sanction Côte d'Ivoire, he hastened. I wonder if Kofi Annan also knew that Chirac was taking advantage of him for the facts of being an African, and a black man at the head of the UN. Or was it that he made a covenant with Chirac for a future assistance in terms of his ambitions in Ghana? So now he was obligated to do his will for the sake of this covenant? Otherwise, what were his reasons for assisting him in his conquest to destroy Côte d'Ivoire?

The creation of the UN (Organization of the United Nations)

Africa has no permanent representative among the five members panel of the Security Council of the UN. Any person would imagine that when on August 31st 1965, membership was brought to 15, with 5 permanent members; at least Africa would have had one (1) representative. But yet, 3 are from Europe, 1 from Asia and 1 from the Americas. So whenever a situation occurs in one African country, there is no one to speak rightfully on its behalf.
When Kofi Annan, another African, a Ghanaian, was nominated after Boutros-Ghali withdrew, and then later Côte d'Ivoire came at odds with France, her erstwhile colonizer, we dauntlessly felt that the new Secretary General would speak on our behalf, if the panel decided otherwise, at least caution the strong man (Chirac) on the basic goals contained in the *Charter of the Organization.*

    1   Peace and security

    2   Fundamental human rights

    3   Justice and respect for international laws

    4   Social progress

    Africa is a victim of its colonization. The African countries are still under colonial influence, even with the declaration of independence; therefore, the justice that the organization is deemed to promote will never be the share of the continent. In the case of Africa, and African countries, the rule of law that applies to them is the will of their master, the colonizer. Even where basic justice needs to be implemented, it is the emotions and feelings of the master that count.

The abusive encounter of Côte d'Ivoire with France and UN in November 2004 should be a wake up call.

The French resolution 1721, read by Kofi Annan:

The French resolution presented to the Security Council of the UN for adoption by Chirac. What ensued made us conclude that the General Secretary of the organization: Kofi Annan was resolute to serving Chirac, and not the UN.

He said the following:
"The new period of the political transition in Côte d'Ivoire *should be the shortest possible and it should constitute the last one given to the rulers of that country before they are discarded."* in a report published on Wednesday November 1st 2006.

Resolution 1721:
"   The Security Council is extending for one more year the period of transition in Côte d'Ivoire until elections are held. Given all power to lead the peace process, the Prime Minister Charles Konan Banny will start the identification operation of voters. Due to the persistence of the crisis in Côte d'Ivoire, and the impossibility to respect the initial electoral calendar, the Council this afternoon has adopted a resolution designed to fully implement the peace process in this country, in order to organize liberal, open, regular, and transparent Presidential and Legislative elections by October 31st, 2007. Presented by France, the resolution 1721 (2006) was unanimously adopted by the 15 members of the Council. Acting in virtue of the chapter VII of the chart of the United Nations, the Council declares that the integral   (total) application of the above resolution, and the peace process under the leadership of the Prime Minister, Mr. Charles Konan Banny, requires of the Ivorian parties to abide fully by its application, without referring to any legal disposition (the constitution) to create an obstacle to the peace process......"

Being unable to write the full report, I sorted the most crucial points.
"# 12 – Requests the immediate resumption of the disarmament program on the entire territory, emphasizes that this program is an

essential element of the peace process…..

13 – Asking the Prime Minister to immediately take all measures by ordinance according to paragraph 8 of the resolution, to speed up the deliverance of the certificates of birth and nationality to **all foreigners**.

29 – Asking instantly neighboring countries to prohibit all movement of fighters or weapons across their borders in direction to Côte d'Ivoire.

32 - The Security Council is ready to impose tough sanctions on any person designated by the committee as hindrance to the peace process in accordance with the paragraph # **14** of the 1572 resolution of (2004) including attacking or any action viewed as an obstacle to the action of the UN and French troops in the country."

The Secretary General Kofi Annan declares that:

"We have to inform the Ivorian leaders that if the transition has been extended this time, this is the last time. If they fail to hold the elections in 2007, the African Union, ECOWAS, and the Security Council will be compelled to establish a governmental structure for a new transition composed of neutral people from the civil society. First of all, the past and present resolutions of the Council, the decisions of the AU and the ECOWAS and peace accords **prevail on the Ivorian constitution and the legality of Côte d'Ivoire.**

Secondly, **the Prime Minister** will exercise his authority on all the services of the state, including the army. Also the leaders of the army and the country are responsible for any obstacle that may occur. The Council will impose sanctions on them, and in the extreme, indict them in international criminal court. Also the Prime Minister will take any decision **without restriction**. Finally, for the success of the peace process, the articles **35** and **48** of the constitution will not be referred to during the period of transition. The UN has to play an accrued role in the key programs, and the Council has to review the mandate of the troops, and give them additional resources."

Blasphemous; this constitutional coup d'état of France against President Laurent Gbagbo of Côte d'Ivoire was sticking out like a sore thumb. In that resolution 1721, the giddy Prime Minister was the new Head of State. The French Licorne troops were also given power to attack Côte d'Ivoire along with the rebels, and no neighboring country was supposed to get involved by sending in fighters or weapons to assist Côte d'Ivoire. As for the rebels, they were entitled to get supplies of weapons through Burkina Faso, or from the troops stationed in the country, and even recruit fighters from other countries to destroy Côte d'Ivoire. That was acceptable because it was the will of Chirac. Chirac and Kofi Annan knew why there could be no elections in the country since 2005. They had decided not to disarm their rebels, and put pressure on President Laurent Gbagbo until they force him out of power. Kofi Annan declared that UN resolutions are above the Ivorian constitution.

I am sure he knew exactly what he was talking about. If these UN resolutions could override the constitution of Côte d'Ivoire, they could also override the constitution of France. Furthermore, they argued that the articles 35 and 48 of the Ivorian constitution should not be referred to during the transitional period; the very article that bestowed illegibility to Alassane for the upcoming Presidential Elections.

Technically speaking, this chapter was closed. The candidacy of Alassane Ouattara had just been hereby revoked by Chirac and Kofi Annan.

NB: for the Ivorian people, the constitution was in full effect; but for Chirac, Alassane Ouattara and Annan, it would remain suspended as they asked for it.

•

I hereby praise the United States, China, Russia, South Africa, Tanzania, and England, who vetoed this resolution 1721 drafted by Chirac, to thwart the coup d'état of France.

"This resolution is affecting the sovereignty of Côte d'Ivoire," said the US Ambassador to the UN, **John Bolton.** In response to the letter of the French resolution against Côte d'Ivoire, the US

Ambassador to the UN, **John Bolton**, on behalf of the United States, China, Russia, and Tanzania disapproved the principle of international texts, such as UN resolutions prevailing on the Ivorian constitution. Furthermore, he said: "Striping the President of Côte d'Ivoire, President Laurent Gbagbo off all his powers conferred to him by the constitution to transfer them to the Prime Minister, is equivalent to a constitutional coup d'état," that, they would not back up such resolution.

An outraged South African UN Ambassador, **Dimisani Kumalo** said: "This is a regime change by the Security Council," and he added: "They would never do that to a European country."

•

Chirac's plan was to tie up President Laurent Gbagbo and prevent him from applying the Ivorian constitution that gives him full executive power like every other President in the world, including Chirac himself. He considers himself as human, compared to President Gbagbo simply because he is a black man. He can chain him, take his constitutional powers away and redirect them to the next black man who can do his will. He knows so much the psychology of the African people that it is easy for him to turn them against each other by dictating his thoughts to the most receptive minds. He knows that many are the traitors against their own countries and continent. He knows they can easily overlook the truth and entertain lies to please the white boy without considering, or being alarmed by the sufferings of their own people. Chirac is not willing to give up his idea of going after the President of Côte d'Ivoire. He knew in his mind that he could never do that to a European country, or even to a country from the Middle East. I would think that Kofi Annan would speak on behalf of an African country such as Côte d'Ivoire in difficult time such as this. At least reason Chirac on the basic things concerning the value and the importance of the constitution of a country. Regardless whether it is a black country or a European country, the constitution serves the same purpose. I am sure Mr. Annan knows what a constitution means in the life of any country. I am also sure that before he was appointed Secretary General of the UN, he passed the basic test of the knowledge of the common things. But to stand before the panel to say the following, including the suspension of the Ivorian constitution, is a disaster to the UN. I almost fainted when I heard Kofi Annan say that:

"All UN resolutions are above the laws of Côte d'Ivoire."

The power of the UN does not have a particular effect on Côte d'Ivoire alone, but should be exercised equitably to all countries members of the organization.

As much as I respect the countries members of the UN, I am at peace today because I am convinced Mr. Annan did not speak on behalf of them. He spoke to please his boy, Chirac, disregarding his career and the consequences thereof. The UN, at this point declines all responsibilities.

Excerpts from News Medias:

1- According to **BBC News**:

"A UN peacekeeping mission failed to achieve disarmament and clashes intensified."

2- The Examiner: Wednesday, December 6, 2006

Kofi Annan: Hussein's best friend at the U.N.

The truth is that Annan's tenure as Secretary General has accomplished little of good anywhere in the world.

" Difficult as it is to believe; it is true that Kofi Annan, head of the preeminent international organization devoted to spreading peace and freedom around the world, thinks that things were better for the average Iraqi when Saddam Hussein was in power.

Here's what Annan, who is leaving his post as U.N. Secretary General at the end of 2006 after serving a decade, told BBC earlier this week.

"If I were an average Iraqi, obviously I would make the same comparison that they had a dictator who was brutal but they had their streets, they could go out, their kids could go to school and come back home without a mother or father worrying: Am I going to see my child again?"

Hey, so what if your relatives could disappear in the night, never to be seen again because Saddam's henchmen tortured and then killed him. Never mind that your neighbor could settle an old score with you by feeding lies to Saddam's neighboring spies.
Never mind that you risked everything, including your life, your job, your family just by whispering to a family member something that could be misconstrued as even remotely critical of Saddam – whose portrait once adorned every Iraqi street corner.

None of these things matters because at least you could walk the streets in safety, according to Annan. .....This is after all the same Annan we know from the UN oil for food scandal in which hundreds of millions of dollars worth of oil revenues were supposed to buy food and medicine for the Iraqi people instead ended up in Saddam's pockets and some of his vicious and corrupt sons.

The truth is that Annan's tenure as Secretary General has accomplished little of good anywhere in the world. U.N. peacekeepers stood by, doing nothing; as Hezbollah launched hundred of rockets to kill innocent Israelis, and raped women and children in Congo DRC without fear of being punished. It is no wonder that the U.N.'s prestige is likely at its lowest ebb ever, especially among the American people who pay most of the U.N.'s bills. Which leaves only one question – Why is Annan waiting until December 31st to leave?"

His Excellency President Laurent Gbagbo, President of Côte d'Ivoire addresses the Ivorian people in reference to the French resolution 1721 presented to the Security Council.
"   The Security Council of the United Nations has just made the resolution 1721 (2006) concerning Côte d'Ivoire. This resolution is the 19th of the kind through which our universal organization is looking into the crisis that shakes Côte d'Ivoire since September 19th 2002. I have the duty to give account of the

circumstances of the above resolution; what it implies, and the victory once again of Côte d'Ivoire and all the African nations.

You know that last year at the same time, the ECOWAS made recommendations concerning the settlement of the Ivorian crisis. A decision was made during a meeting of its Peace and Security Council. In reference to that decision, I decided to make no comments. After that the UN was called in to close the procedure.

Like me, you learned about a draft of resolution that was used as a basis of the work of the Security Council of the UN.
This project contained a dangerous affirmation which stipulated: "The decisions of the Security Council of the UN prevail on the Ivorian constitution and the legalization of the country." This affirmation was raising the double questions of the sovereignty of the independent African States, and the legality of these states compared to other states of the world. On this fundamental question, the UN ruled out: Clearly, the countries members of the Security Council rejected all possibility of the subordination of the constitution of any state, to a decision of an international institution, should it be the UN. Our country is pleased to have given the Security Council the occasion to settle that matter. We are happy for ourselves, but also for all the countries of the world yearning for freedom.

I am taking this opportunity to salute the super powers, members of the Security Council of the United Nations who share with us the same conception of the constitution and the sovereignty. I salute their belief in the loyalty of the chart of the United Nations, and to the spirit that they just gave to the people of the world. The position of the Security Council has just put an end to the debate on the probability to deny the sovereignty of any state by the suspension or the modification of its constitution by the UN. Therefore, our constitution will be applied.

Dear Ivorian, another debate concerning the possibility of the Prime Minister appointing to key positions in the civil administration as well as in the military was raised. The same project of resolution contained the following paragraph through which the Prime Minister could "appoint to key civil and military positions." This debate was also settled by the same resolution. According to our constitution, the Prime Minister of Côte d'Ivoire who is appointed by the President of the Republic by a decree, can not also appoint by decree. The Prime Minister will never make a nomination to positions either civil or military.

Surely, the above mentioned text being the fruit of a strenuous diplomatic battle, it is our duty, the Ivorian people, beneficiaries of the peace in our country, to pursue and complete this battle that took place at the Security Council on our behalf. That is why all other wording contained in the text that constitutes a violation to our constitution will not be applied. This position, we will defend it because it complies with the question of the national sovereignty of Côte d'Ivoire. We will continue to defend it because we are not the only beneficiaries. This position is profitable to all the independent States of Africa and the world.

Dear Ivorian, I conjure you to go further. We need in fact to work hand in hand to search for peace for our country. I am going to repeat myself; the outsiders can only help regardless of their concern. Thousands resolutions can be written, they will fail if we refuse peace. I am inviting you to be united around our constitution and the institutions of our country. For four years you have been fighting for the survival of Côte d'Ivoire. I am asking you to stand firm. The time has come to take responsibilities. First of all, I am inviting the army at large to protect the populations, and to defend the constitution of the country. I am asking everyone to be calm, and to refrain from every manifestation that those who want the sufferings to continue will take advantage of, and lead the country into the chaos. You may go to work, to your farms, or to your schools.

I gave instructions to the police to watch over the public safety in the district of Abidjan, and on all the national territory. I asked the army to back them up any time when needed so that nothing comes to disturb the necessary measures intended to bring back peace. Let us preserve our constitution and our institutions. Our power in this battle is the solidarity of the sacred bond between the President, the people, and the army. Let us be bonded. In a couple of days I will speak to you again to give you the guidelines of the measures for the settlement of this crisis. **God bless you**.

•

Remarks raised by the French resolution 1721:

Souleymane T. Senn Assistant in Communication, Journalist, said the following:

"Jacques Chirac, the French President, and Jean-Marie De la Sablière, his Ambassador at the UN, have failed at the Security Council to suspend the Ivorian constitution, and [transform the elected President of Côte d'Ivoire, President Laurent Gbagbo, into the Queen of England] and make of Charles Konan Banny, his favorite man, the new Head of State of Côte d'Ivoire through the resolution 1721. This failure is seen by the French diplomacy as a humiliation. Chirac and his accomplices can not get over this, so they are now preparing another plot to avenge themselves against the President of Côte d'Ivoire," we just heard from a source closed to the UN.

•

The UN Ambassador of one country that took part in the negotiations at the Security Council said the following:

"I understand the joy of the Ivorian people as a result of the resolution 1721. It is not over; you have not yet won the war against Chirac."

The resolution 1721 was vetoed by the **United States**, **China**, **Russia**, **Great Britain**, **Tanzania**, and **South Africa**. These countries believe in Democracy, and Human Rights; therefore reject the notion of subordination.

Chapter Eight
President Thabo Mbeki and the mediation
God speaks to me about the liberation of Côte d'Ivoire

I **HEREBY PRAISE GOD** for allowing his son, the Honorable Thabo Mbeki, President of the Republic of South Africa, for getting involved in the resolve of the crisis in Côte d'Ivoire. The role he was called to play since day one is priceless. God Who so much loves the Ivorian people did not stay indifferent, and called his son, His Excellency President Thabo Mbeki to speak on our behalf, knowing that all had turned their back on us, playing the game of Chirac, the colon.

When President Thabo Mbeki was appointed Mediator in the crisis in Côte d'Ivoire by his fellow Presidents of the African Union, all agreed and applauded. The rebels and all the opposition parties that support them, including all the international organizations of which Côte d'Ivoire is a member, approved the nomination of President Thabo Mbeki at the head of the mediation. Since then, he has done a great job. He conducted the negotiations with such honesty, serenity, and determination in spite of the verbal attacks and abuses he has been subject of regularly.

President Thabo Mbeki has proved to the world that he is a great man; a king; and a man of wisdom, knowing the boundary between wrong and right.
He is one of the few leaders that the continent of Africa can count on for its deliverance from oppression, and subjection. He is a man

of integrity. I can see what triggered the Honorable Nelson Mandela's reliance in him and chose him not only to entrust the destiny of his people in his hands, but to pursue elegantly the fight for the liberation of South Africa from the snare of apartheid for which he was jailed 27years.

As a matter of fact, I have never heard him making declarations against any one of the parties involved in the conflict, in spite of the disobedience of many. Because of his influence, and in the spirit of bringing an end to the sufferings of the Ivorian people, the rebels obtained exceptional eligibility of Alassane Dramane Ouattara to the Presidential Elections. The rebels also obtained the management of the radio and television stations, and the majority in the electoral commission, and much more.

In his report of August 2005, President Thabo Mbeki clearly stated that the President of Côte d'Ivoire applied in its entirety all the agreements signed. The report says that among all the under signers, he was the only one to have fully fulfilled his part of incumbencies. On behalf of the Mediator and President of South Africa, his defense Minister brought before the Security Council the report of the Mediation. The report stipulated:
"All the necessary accords designed to leverage all obstacles to the application of the accords have been finalized" and "the decisions that have been made by the Security Council, stating that all the persons making obstruction to the application of the accords will be sanctioned," should be applied.
What the Mediator meant by this is that the only thing remaining to be done is the disarmament of the rebels and the opposition parties that support them constitute the obstacle to the application of the accords, so they should be sanctioned.

The rebels are known to be ruthless and very arrogant. They have no regards for legality, and they have not fulfilled their part of commitment concerning all the accords signed during the peace talks. They have never been sanctioned for that matter. But sanctions are always hanging over the government in case the

President fails to comply with one thing or the other. Today we are witnessing a campaign of intoxication conducted by the rebels, the opposition, and all the outsiders who cater to them and support them. This includes delivering them diplomatic documents, money, and transportation. All the people who applauded when President Thabo Mbeki was first nominated are smearing his name, simply because he has not joined in with them in their dirty work against President Gbagbo, and the destruction of Côte d'Ivoire.

President Thabo Mbeki is sincere and honest. He is a wise man, and a leader the African people can count on to have justice rendered to the afflicted. He is a man who deserves high respect. Through these lines, I vehemently come against whosoever will venture use his name with slightness; anyone, including the African people, or anybody who is attempting to smear the name of his Excellency, President Thabo Mbeki for speaking on behalf of Côte d'Ivoire.

The blood of the innocent babies, women, young men and old, that was shed by the criminals cried; and the prayers of the survivors have reached unto God, triggering his powerful hand to save not only Côte d'Ivoire, but the old French colonies, and the whole continent of Africa.
At one point in time, God chose Moses to free the children of Israel from bondage. Being that He is the same yesterday, today and forever, the time has come to liberate the continent from the clutches of slavery.

God speaks to me on December 28th 2002, at 8:30 PM

I was blessed to hear the voice of God on December 28, 2002 a short time after the brutal attack on Côte d'Ivoire, on my way to a seminary on Spiritual Gifts, with Prophet Eric YAHI. As we were driving on New Hampshire Avenue, under Route 29, the Holy Spirit got hold on me. As he pressed down on me, I heard in a clear voice, the following message:
"**Go and see Pascal,**" *and the Spirit took me to the Ambassador of* Côte d'Ivoire *at that time, Dr. Pascal Kokora,* "**Ask him to call the President,**" *and the Spirit took me to President Laurent*

GBAGBO, "**And transmit my message to him. I want to free Côte d'Ivoire as I did in the old time when the army of Senacherib came against the children of God, I sent one Angel to slay 185,000 enemy soldiers. Go, and transmit my message to him.**" *And the voice withdrew from me as if it was pulled by a spring.*

I was in tears when I became conscious. I did exactly as the Lord commended me to do, in vain. Please God forgive me if I never had the opportunity to transmit your message. You know I did try as I was commanded, but you know, here it is not easy for people to let you speak to the President regardless of the purpose, unless you are one of them. Also in these days there are so many prominent and anointed men of God around the President that, it would be unacceptable that God, the Almighty speaks to an ordinary man like me who is not even a Pastor. So I did come to a dead end road.

I am therefore begging you to find me another way around, if you really want me to still transmit your message; **Amen.**

Chapter Nine
The battle within

PRIOR TO OCTOBER 31st, 2005, the constitutional date for the Presidential election in Côte d'Ivoire, all we heard everyday from the opposition was: "Constitutional void," meaning, comes October 31st, 2005, President Laurent Gbagbo will no longer be the President of Côte d'Ivoire. It became the colloquial slogan of every political party, and the headlines of every Newspaper in the country. The opposition parties even decreed that all the economic operators should not only withdraw from the country, but stop every transaction in connection with the economy of Côte d'Ivoire. And every citizen of the country should stop paying taxes after October 31st, 2005, to denounce the authority of President Laurent Gbagbo. It was just unbelievable to hear and witness such things. What prompted such profound hatred against President Laurent Gbagbo? Was it because they all agreed to suffocate the country once for all, or have it wiped out of the face of the earth because of the tenure of President Gbagbo? What were then the motive and the cause of such deep rooted abhorrence, and animosity towards President Gbagbo? I am strongly hostile to this kind of treatment. I am an advocate of mutual respect among people; and I vehemently oppose any discriminatory act toward others, and despise all contumacious behaviors.

It is so obvious that President Gbagbo and the majority of the Ivorian politicians do not believe in the same thing, nor see things the same way. That is why throughout the crisis, the dialogue between President Gbagbo and the opposition seemed like talking to aliens on a different planet. And the opposition at large was treating him exactly as would a Hyena lost in a herd of lions be treated. From this scene you could tell that some of us chose to entertain falsehood purposely.

For President Gbagbo, time has evolved; the colonial era is obsolete. We need to be ourselves and rely on ourselves in order to develop our countries. We have the resources and the manpower. All we need is to lay down the goals, the objectives, and get to work to have things done. Our children have grown, so we need to create opportunities for them and for the future generations. This means; cutting the colonial ties, and minimizing the financial burden payable to the colonizer in reference to those old contracts. This surplus of money will come to us and will allow us to undertake major investments. We will create opportunities for our citizens, our youths, the growing generations, and develop our country at the same time. We know that no colonizer can do this for us. For the Ivorian opposition, even though we have the resources and the manpower, we have to continue to depend on the colonizer. We have to remain where we were before the 60's. There is no point of getting out of colonialism. We can continue to rent from France the palaces of the Presidency and the National Assembly. We can continue to pay the 65 per cent of our yearly revenue to France as before in accordance with the colonial contracts. We can continue to be underdeveloped, and remain a third world continent indefinitely. As long as we, the politicians are happy, it does not matter if the rest of the population lives in deprivation. This is the scope of the battle within. Besides this, President Gbagbo has not done anything wrong to anyone, to be treated like an intruder in his own country.

We were surprised to know that the main topics of the meeting of Marcoussis revolved around three points:
1- **Alassane Ouattara's** candidacy,
2- **The Presidential Election**, and

3- The power of the Prime Minister.

From the above topics, we began to understand who was behind this coup d'état, and why it was launched. President Gbagbo was the target. Now they wanted elections because they failed to achieve their goal nightly. For us, elections are for normal people. You can not subscribe to coups d'état, fail, and then turn around and claim elections; it is either one or the other, but not both at the same time. Those who do not want to go through elections are the ones who subscribe to coups d'états. The enemies of Côte d'Ivoire knew that an election could never be held in any civilized country under these circumstances; a country divided in two, with rebels controlling the North, and the government controlling the South. The UN was well aware of those hampering circumstances. The AU and the ECOWAS were conscious of those obstacles that constituted hindrance for holding the Presidential election. They all knew the actual and fragile condition of the country in terms of acting upon an election, but they still pressed upon it. Some of us were outraged about this treatment, including President Laurent Gbagbo who always thought that his neighbors and fellow Africans were with him in this crisis. He eventually lost hope but did not rest upon it. He ended up writing to the President of the AU, President Olusugun Obasanjo, expressing his concern:

President Laurent Gbagbo writes to
President Olusugun Obasanjo.

"**The Courier of Abidjan**" **October 2005,** the resolution 1633 was misleading by focusing more on the Prime Minister power, without mentioning the disarmament of the rebels.

Excellency,
"I have read a draft of resolution concerning the Ivorian crisis dated October 13, 2005, which will be submitted for review to the Security Council. I have made remarks on the significant paragraphs of the draft of resolution.

I am sending to your care Ambassador Sarata Touré Ottro Zirignon, my under director of Cabinet to bring you the draft of the resolution and the remarks that I made thereof.

In addition to those documents, I would like to address my concerns regarding the Ivorian crisis in which you have invested so much in months. I would like first of all to underline that this draft allocated too much space on the issues related to the Prime Minister.

However, today this is not the most important thing to get out of the crisis in Côte d'Ivoire. The important question, in terms of obstacles to come out of the crisis is the disarmament.

I would like to say that should only bear weapons in Côte d'Ivoire persons who bear them legally. These persons are members of the National Army, the Gendarmerie and the National Police as well as those of the National Guard and the Water and Forestry. Every other persons, should it be the rebels or the groups of self defense, should be absolutely disarmed in order to give Côte d'Ivoire her freedom and her safety, and for the protection of properties and persons.

Afterward, once the disarmament is made, we should immediately organize the Presidential elections as soon as possible. In fact, the sooner the elections will be organized, the better Côte d'Ivoire will be. Finally, concerning the elections besides the Presidential, the resolution can be pleased to say that every other election will be postponed as many times as it will take to organize the Presidential elections.

Therefore, wanting to dwell more on the issue of the Prime Minister, we tend to ignore the real problems. The failure of the out going Prime Minister is not because of the fact that he lacked powers. They were given to him and he accepted them during the conference of Accra on July 29 and 30, of 2004, and during the conference of Pretoria in April 2005. His failure is not because of his supposedly antagonism with the President of the Republic.

Each one of us has an area perfectly defined by the constitution and by the accords that were signed. The failure of the outgoing Prime Minister is the result of the dates he set for the disarmament himself or by the different peace accords that have not been honored by the rebels. The later ones have so much personal interests that they oppose any attempt of normalization of the situation in Côte d'Ivoire.

Therefore today, what the Ivorian people and I, myself are expecting from the international community is to boldly condemn the rebels' refusal to disarm. The international community has to indicate the necessary measures to take in order to disarm the rebels so that the liberties and safety be reinstalled in Côte d'Ivoire, and for the elections to take place as soon as possible. Disarmament, Elections: these are the two points on which the debate should be centered."

The President of the Republic of Côte d'Ivoire, **President Laurent Gbagbo**.

Chapter Ten
Peace and Freedom / The ladder of evolution

To the Ivorian opposition and the G7

PEACE IS NEVER achieved with malicious lips.

- You can never achieve peace when you are burning villages, killing babies, and wiping out entire families.

- More less through the hose of a Kalashnikov.

- Never, when you maintain your country divided in two, and you strive to reinforce the stronghold of the rebels, asking them not to disarm.

- What kind of peace are you talking about when you are driving all economic operators out of the country; asking them to stop all transactions with Côte d'Ivoire? Supposedly your own country. What kind of peace are you imploring when you are asking your fellow citizens to stop paying taxes to the country, and calling for a national disobedience to the government?

Just in case you are not aware of this; Peace is the fruit of the seeds of dialogue and non- violence. Peace comes from the practice of Love - the Love of **Jesus Christ** – that we are all created equal – all children of **God**, with equal opportunities. So In the case of the Presidency, this means that when your brother comes in power, you should not disturb him because in politics everyone should have a turn. Everybody can not be President at the same time. Also, the country is a public property, belonging to every child, son and daughter of the nation. In the country, every son and daughter have their personal properties over which they do exercise every right. They can freely decide who may be admitted on their properties, and when they should exercise the rule of trespassing.

Côte d'Ivoire is not the personal property of a political party, an ethnic group or a tribe, an individual, more less a colon. The President of Côte d'Ivoire, President Laurent Gbagbo who was elected on October 31st 2000, did not trespass on anyone's property. He did not violate anyone's right; so legally, no one has the right to ask him to step down without elections being held.

The political opposition and the rebels are crying for peace, while they are not making any efforts leading to peace. My understanding is that you want peace at your convenience, provided that President Gbagbo should leave power. God is the witness as he is making all the consensuses, and yielding to most of their requests just for the sake of peace. No one has the right to impose his will on the Ivorian people, or ask President Gbagbo to step down unless that individual can prove that he is the proprietor of Côte d'Ivoire, or the creator of the Ivorian people; or he or she is more Ivorian than the rest of us, or better fit for the Presidency than anyone else. We all have equal opportunities and equal rights in the country. So for your knowledge, I would like to inform you that the real peace that the Ivorian people needs and deserves is in the mighty hands of our **Lord Jesus Christ**; not in your blood stained hands.

Our Father God has already promised to set the country free. When he does, you will see and also benefit from this freedom; even though you intended to destroy the country, we will not hold you accountable. God being merciful, He sends rain and makes the sun shine on both the righteous and the gentiles - the children of the Living God as well as the Moabites. I can see the day is coming when every knee shall bow; the knees of the colon Chirac, Alassane Ouattara, Bédié, Djédje Mady, Soro and company shall bow; and every tongue shall confess; the tongue of Chirac, Alassane Ouattara, Bédié, Djédjé Mady, Soro and company, even though smeared with innocent blood, shall confess that Jesus Christ is Lord and Savior.

We may never disclaim our creator in heaven. As for our colonizer, we can dispel him anytime, and that time is now. Although we are well aware that breaking from him will cost us; we will never falter because freedom is vital; it is the prerequisite for the uplifting of Africa, and our countries. I believe that our Lord and father will take us through every step of the way to the "Promise Land"; the land of freedom.

I pledge this day:

It is time for the African people to start organizing themselves and setting real goals, and reachable objectives in terms of pulling Africa out of the snare of colonialism.
It takes unerring efforts, determination, dedication, sacrifices, and all the human qualities and resources to reach perfection. Therefore, my pledge to the African people today is that they should begin to lay down the foundation of a true organization of all the African countries in the continent. Strength comes from unity; not **individualism**. Individualism implies **vulnerability** and **weakness**. We are in the era of globalization, so for Africa to occupy a seat around the table of super powers, we need to pull together in order to strengthen Africa economically, politically, as well as militarily. And the only way to get to that level is through true "UNITY."

Other people pulled together and it worked; so why can't

we do it also for ourselves. Nothing is impossible if you are determined. Things become complicated and impossible when you take no initiatives.

For instance, when you take a look at history, you find out that it took the United States of America about two centuries to be free and get united. Considering their success story, you can see that it took planning, determination, hard working and dedicated people who were willing to make the sacrifices. But the bottom line is, they decided for themselves, and their efforts paid off. That is why it is important for the African people to seek freedom first.

Also it took the Europeans more than one century after Spain brought up the idea of Unity in order to get where they are today. Even though they still have a lot to accomplish, let us note that it did not happen overnight, nor fall on them from the sky unexpectedly like sow falling in winter. They made the commitment and they stuck to it. So the African people need to make plans in that direction; at least pave the way for the freedom of future generations. There are no more excuses to continue to sit back and pretend everything is normal.

Unless the African people expresses the need for the freedom of Africa, and starts laying down comprehensive plans to come out of colonialism, people like Chirac will never have respect and consideration for the continent of Africa, the African people, and the resources of the continent.

In other words, he takes advantage of the behavior of the African leaders to impose his will on the continent.

The power hungry:

Many are the power hungry who refuse to follow the proper procedures in the conquest of power. They infiltrate weapons in our countries for their personal interests. They organize coup d'états, wars and rebellions, killing innocent people to seek power instead of using the money they bought the weapons with to create factories and jobs for the youths. In this case, are we going to accuse the outsiders for killing us? I don't think so. The African people need to review their own ways and behaviors, and seek to get close to God if they want peace in Africa, and if they want the outsiders to respect the continent, its inhabitants, its values and resources.

Côte d'Ivoire:

At one point during the crisis in Côte d'Ivoire we had the impression that the President of Côte d'Ivoire committed such a terrible crime for which he was personally held accountable, that now he and all his supporters and sympathizers: the patriots and a part of the population had to pay with their lives. Pressure came from everywhere pending on the government, President Gbagbo and his supporters, making them look like *criminals isolated in a correctional facility on a remote island where they had to await the death penalty.*
The picture of the whole scenario evinced as follows:

The plaintiff:

Jacques Chirac, President of France, all his allies including: the Ivorian opposition, the Northern part of the country with the local rebels, the AU, the ECOWAS, and the UN; the union of all the nations of the world.

Vs.
The accused:

President Laurent Gbagbo, the government of Côte d'Ivoire, the patriots, and sympathizers. **The crime committed by the accused:**
The accused intended to break the colonial ties, revoke the contracts of yore, stop paying the colonial overheads, and claim the total independence of his country.

The plaintiff's charges against the accused:

The plaintiff intends to keep the colonial contracts in full force, continue to advocate his influence as a colonial master, and control the economy of the country indefinitely.
The economy of his own country has always been based on the performance of his colonies. He does not believe in the freedom and independence of none of his colonies. He can not afford losing

money, so any President who will initiate questioning the colonial contracts' existence becomes automatically his enemy. This is a matter of life and death. "Either you stay in power and do according to the contracts or you get toppled or you die and you get replaced by the right person willing to play the game of interests."

In terms of the account payable in reference of the colonial overheads, Côte d'Ivoire was very juicy. In addition to the big accounts, the leasing of some estates such as: the palaces of the National Assembly, the Presidency, and probably many more landmarks were not negligible. I am certain when President Laurent Gbagbo took office and he discovered these kinds of transactions between France and our country, he became outraged. A patriot can barely put up with this so he certainly took corrective actions. This is the main reason why Chirac hates President Laurent Gbagbo so much, and he ordered the coup d'état to oust him on September 19[th,] 2002, in order to position someone who would help him maintain and enforce the colonial deals. His right person remained hidden as the killers executed the coup on September 19th 2002. No one would have ever known who was behind it if they had succeeded and taken over. Then his theory of "internal conflict" would have been justified.

Quote:

Former Prime Minister Tony Blair of England referred to President Laurent Gbagbo as: "a great and intelligent politician."

He said the following in the Economist News Magazine:
"*International politics should not be simply a game of interests, but also of beliefs; things we stand for and fight for.*" **The economist,** dated: June 2nd 2007.

Throughout the crisis in Côte d'Ivoire, you could tell that all the African leaders favored Chirac's cause. Signs extricated out of their behavior as though they did not believe in the freedom of their respective countries. They were acting as if they had a pending covenant with the former colonizer. During the peace talks and various meetings, you could see the African Leaders beating about the bush. They dealt with Soro Guillaume, the chief rebel as if he was a Head of State. They rolled the red carpet before him, and cherished him as the "prodigal child" of the king. None of them mentioned or condemned the atrocities he inflicted on the Ivorian population, or showed some kind of concern for their sufferings. We heard them talking and drafting measures to get out of the crisis. They wrote hundreds of accords, and passed numerous resolutions to no avail. When the President of Côte d'Ivoire, President Laurent Gbagbo mentioned the issue of the disarmament of the rebels, they simply called the meetings a day, making it look like his request was irrelevant. They portrayed him as if he did not fit in their herd. They probably tried to send him a message as an encrypted data, but he was unable to decode it.

I was informed that each one of the African Leaders would call him in the middle of the night to encourage him and tell him to continue to challenge Chirac.
"We know what is going on, and we understand the scope of your battle; but you know we can not back you up openly otherwise our power will be at risk," they would say to him. I am sorry, and I hate to say this, but that is called hypocrisy. If we intend to lift up our continent, our leaders need to rise above their selfish interests, and stop making hypocritical calculations. They need to be inspired by President Laurent Gbagbo's experience in Côte d'Ivoire.

As Lucky Dube sings: "**When you go up the ladder, treat the people who helped you right, because the day you come down, you will need them.**"
The Ivorian people protected President Laurent Gbagbo when he was attacked because he loves them, and they know what he wants to accomplish for them. But when you keep your people in abject poverty and you walk over their heads and lie to them, you can only be hypocrite because you know the day that France comes

against you; they will not risk their lives to protect you.

The African Leaders need to understand that Freedom is never voluntarily given by the oppressor. It must be demanded by the oppressed, though freedom has always been an expensive thing to obtain. History is a testimony to the fact that freedom is rarely obtained without sacrifice.

During his time of opposition, President GBAGBO taught the Ivorian people that they were not independent.
"Even though we achieved independence in 1960, it was never real and total. Our country is still tied to its former colonizer France, by "cooperation contracts" in the form of a modernized version of colonialism," he asserted.

While in this conditions, we cannot exercise the right of freedom, or even say that we are independent. Independence means that we no longer "depend" on he who once served as an overseer, a trainer or a parent. In other words, the formerly dependent individual or country, is now on his or its own, and is now free to make his or its own decisions. So to me it is not acceptable that a country that is said to be **"independent"** be still under colonial influence. In Africa, all the countries that were formerly French colonies, even after they achieved independence are still under colonial influence, compared to countries that were colonized by England. The formerly English colonies in Africa are now independent countries. During the colonial era, whatever the colonized countries produced through the efforts of their farmers was produced for the benefit of the colonizer. These products were considered the property of the colonizer. After the achievement of the independence, this practice has not changed. That is why the Ivorian coffee is labeled **"French Coffee"** in all the Super Markets around the world. Even though we know that France does not cultivate nor produce coffee and cocoa on its soil. As the colonizer, or slave owner, whatever the slave produces belongs to the master. So by Côte d'Ivoire being the world's biggest producer of coffee and cocoa, it is the name of France that appears on world markets;

not the name of Côte d'Ivoire. This is one of the many rules of servitude. No country can go around it unless that country breaks the backbone of colonialism.

Another rule of servitude is that a slave master can never order the freedom of his slave. The slave has to get up and express the need for his freedom. In many cases the slaves always ran away, and when they were caught, they paid the hard way. Some slaves were simply hanged when caught, or they had one leg cut off to prevent them from escaping again; according to how the master felt that day.

The former slave called "Côte d'Ivoire" led by the FPI, and President Gbagbo, decided to escape from the master, so to speak. Therefore the master reacted vehemently and expressed his discontentment in November 2004, killing many of the slave's children; the patriots. The master was very angry because without Côte d'Ivoire he can not balance his budget. His economy was always based on the performance of the slave. This rule applies to all the former French colonies in Africa.

In the case of Côte d'Ivoire, I can understand that France cannot afford to lose complete control of it, as Côte d'Ivoire is a very precious country which plays a huge role in the economy of France. Therefore, wouldn't it be wise for Chirac to negotiate diplomatically with the country's government by using a polite tone of voice, a respectful and good manner? Perhaps with such attitude, we, the Ivorian people would have agreed to pay some dues; something just to help out, even if it would be much less than the total colonial overheads we have been paying to France for many years or decades. As a longtime partner of France, we would not turn our back on her abruptly in retaliation to the way Chirac has been treating us, and especially the way he treated us in November 2004. We would not do that because culturally speaking, the Ivorian people are very tolerant and forgiving. We would have poured water in our wine instead of keeping it strong, so to speak, and:

1- Seek to revise and configure the colonial covenants which keep us infinitely in a position of servitude, and change that man-made condition into a real partnership with France.

2- Update the relationship between our two countries, and establish a true cooperative friendship. Whatever did not apply would be taken out, like the military bases without military accords; and whatever did not exist would be added, like the freedom to hire contractors based on price. 3- Proclaim our independence from our former colonizer, and create a new environment to work as friends and partners, instead of: "Master and Slave."

Unfortunately, with the choice Chirac has subscribed to, we can see he is not ready to back off, revise his position, and give up the harassments. Using brutality as if we owe France is the type of injustice that can only be advocated on the continent of Africa, due to our own behaviors.

Côte d'Ivoire is a nation with its territory, his population, and its government; a nation that is free to have partners in terms of interdependence. In this new millennium, no country (rich or poor, black or white) should still have to crawl under colonial rules. We believe that this issue can be solved through dialogue and diplomacy only by prioritizing the welfare of the Ivorian people, the African people, and setting aside all personal interests. Although we subscribe both to dialogue and diplomacy, we are strongly committed to getting our freedom, and our total independence. No circumstances of brutality or intimidation of any sort, shape or form will ever divert us from our stance, or deter us from pursuing what is best for our country, our population, and for our continent. At this point, Chirac has only one alternative if he wants to retain our friendship. However, if he persists on his manhunt, indecent behavior and criminal activities towards the Ivorian people, and continues to advocate his supremacy, and refuses to revise his ways, we will assume that: [**Chirac has implicitly subscribed to France's dismissal from Côte d'Ivoire, and probably from all the African; countries.**] Although this is not the only option opened to to him; nevertheless, the choice is his.

My position about relationships:

Breaking relationship with any country is not the best thing to do. Though countries are independent, or aspire to some kind of freedom as an independent entity, no country is self sufficient on its own. All countries are **INTERDEPENDENT** in a global system. I will never encourage the breaking of relations between two countries, whether it is with a former colonizer misbehaving or not. At the same time I will not tolerate infringement upon any country's sovereignty, whether it is a poor or a former colonial country. I am an advocate of mutual respect and justice among individuals, and nations. Concerning the crisis between France and Côte d'Ivoire, it is up to the French to decide whether she wants to keep a sound relationship with us based on respect.

As for Côte d'Ivoire, she has no problem being France's best friend as she has always been. All we are pressing upon is respect as a country, instead of brutality and inferior treatment as would a slave be treated.

Every country has the right to develop itself by utilizing its own resources or outsource in some instances. It deserves to be free and assure protection of its population, or defend itself in the event of an aggression, and develop liberal relations with other countries. No country's resources should be declared the property of another country. What the French colonies in Africa are going through is inadmissible and intolerable. All the African countries colonized by France are undergoing issues of rebellion, genocide and other inhuman circumstances. That is why I conjure all the leaders and all the African people who may be concerned by my call and my pledge, whether they dwell in Africa or abroad, to join in with the cause of Côte d'Ivoire, and President Laurent Gbagbo in order to fight for the suppression of colonialism in Africa.

The ultimate wish of a President:
President Laurent Gbagbo wishes the end of the rebellion

and the crisis in Côte d'Ivoire. He wishes to see his country unified as before in order to have the Presidential Elections as a civilized country. He wishes that things become normal again as they were when President Houphouët Boigny was the commander in chief. He wishes that Côte d'Ivoire becomes a role model of development and peace in the region so that investors and economic operators can feel safe to come in to create jobs for the youths, knowing that politicians don't. He wishes the best for his country. He went out of his way to negotiate directly with the local rebels, asking them to come home if they would. President Gbagbo's endeavor throughout this crisis has been outstanding, and I personally support him on every road he took, although my views about dealing with rebellion remain undeterred. We all hope that his long sufferings yield the expected results so that Côte d'Ivoire can retrieve its peace and freedom. This is what President Laurent Gbagbo wants for his country while his opponents are on a different mission. On the other hand, what do Chirac and Kofi Annan want?

Certainly they do not want peace in Côte d'Ivoire. If they did, the course of their actions would surely indicate it. Chirac wants President Gbagbo out of power so he can install his favorite man. And until he removes him, he will maintain the rebels in position, continue to provide them with weapons and necessities, enforce the line of partition of the country with the Licorne troops, and promote international pressure on the Ivorian government. This conspiracy is so plain and well crafted that people like me refuse to be distracted by their so called peace process. If we would ever make the mistake to let President Gbagbo step aside for one week, and observe them, they would place their man and declare the end of the crisis, and then validate the constitution. But are we stupid enough to do that, and grant them that luxury?

Since Chirac knows the psychology of the African people, his strategy in Africa is to utilize the most ignorant and receptive ones against the maverick, like President Laurent Gbagbo of Côte d'Ivoire.

Two battles to win

For instance in November 2004, after his devastating and disproportionate act of retaliation, he subsequently requested Kofi Annan's help at the UN in order to sanction the government of Côte d'Ivoire. His plan was to make sure that President Laurent Gbagbo would not buy new weapons in replacement of the ones he destroyed. And Kofi Annan played that role very well. He did not hesitate to please his friend by imposing a weapon ban on the Ivorian government, leaving the attackers (the rebels) out. He even extended the sanctions to the patriots, the First Lady, the President of the National Assembly, and the President of the FPI, party in power. Literally, they displayed their intimacy to the rebels.

Chirac knows that many of our African brothers have no class. They are always ready to play his game and please him regardless of the circumstances. He knows that many are those who are ready to kill for a bundle of Euros. That is why he thinks he is the master over the continent of Africa; because we let him be the master. In his evil plan to oust President Gbagbo, he had accomplices he could rely on in Africa, in Côte d'Ivoire as well as at the UN. This plan had not been so conspicuous anywhere else, and he had never encountered such resistance anywhere else either. The bottom line is; Chirac and Kofi Annan are not for peace in Côte d'Ivoire or anywhere else in Africa.

What does the Ivorian opposition want? Needless to ask that question; they want President Gbagbo out simply because he intends to change things in the country that will no longer favor the old culture and practices. His program will also create a lot of opportunities and eventually the Ivorian people will be happy and be attached to him. This is one thing that scares them because they do not have the mind to create opportunities. They just want to be in power to show off, run around in SUV's like young boys playing with their toys, and then feed the rest of us with speeches.

Even though they may be educated, the thing they lack is innovation, intelligence, wisdom and love for their nation. The problem of Africa is a constant battle between Intelligence, and Education. Africa has as many educated men and women as the

Daman Laurent Adjehi - 125 -

developed world. But I have to say this: Intelligence is contrary to Education.

Intelligence is the ability to look at a fact, grasp a clear conception of it, analyze it and come up with a reasonable conclusion. Intelligence gives you the ability to innovate, create for the benefit of all, and it gives you discernment to differentiate between wrong and right. When you are intelligent, you set yourself in the light of creative altruism.

We have always had kings, chiefs of regions and villages who were highly intelligent and wise, but never sat on a school chair their entire lives. If these kings and chiefs were associated with the political life of their countries, they would not be easily manipulated, corrupted, or driven into selling their countries at auction because these men had integrity. They could make good advisers for African leaders, but no leader consult them on critical issues.

Now, when you are only educated from books, and you lack intelligence and wisdom, you constantly remain in the darkness of destructive selfishness. You then entertain lies and engage in groundless conversations, proving that you are the truth bearer. Most of the time within your inner self, you know it is a lie; but for selfish gains and egoism, you stick to it and you fiercely hate counter views. That is exactly the path chosen by the G7 association; those who claim to be heirs of the man who worked hard his entire life for the development of Côte d'Ivoire. This man, President Houphouët Boigny, was a prince of peace in Africa, and a man of dialogue.

Although he launched a couple of times some extirpating and repressive offensives on designated groups in retaliation, he still preached peace. And although he did not fully take us out of the yoke of French colonialism, he knew the time would come for our freedom. How then in the world, did his sons and heirs choose to turn their back on dialogue, and have subscribed to rebellion? Thus disrupting the peace their father had built, and instilled in the minds of the Ivorian as well as the African people? Asking the rest of the Ivorian people to think, and act like them?

President Gbagbo's problem with his internal enemies is that he wants to take the country out from where it is, and position it where it ought to be, whereas they don't seem to see it that way. They want to play the game of Chirac, and France, our former colonizer forever. I am personally ire that President Gbagbo has become the scapegoat; being blamed for every problem he did not create. For instance the term "**Ivoirité**" that brought all the confusion and the misunderstanding in the country, was created even before President he took office; but he is blamed by some for drowning the country. Many have quickly forgotten their past. Instead of feeling sorry for their sloppy and negligent leadership, they put the blame on others who have nothing to do with it. I strongly believe that if America had been under French Influence, it would not be developed as it is today. President Houphouët knew that there is time for everything. What he did is what he could do at that time.
He knew that there were enough intelligent people among the Ivorian people who would think critically and do the things he couldn't do during his time span. He knew that the time of servitude would end one day; not by itself, but by his children taking actions, political or diplomatic, or even fighting for its suppression. African countries are not the only countries that were under foreign influence. America was once under British influence. I strongly believe that if America had been under French Influence, it would not be developed as it is today.

When President Houphouët achieved the first proclamation of independence on August 7th, 1960, he knew that it was not a full independence, but simply a process; and the second phase would be undertaken by his sons after he would be gone. He probably saw something in Bédié that made him chose him as his direct heir over all the Ivorian children, if it wasn't only to perpetuate his ideology and cover up the mistakes that he did not want the Ivorian people to discover. However, if it was for the right cause, had he been here today, he would surely have regretted his choice for Bédié. He would have noticed the failure he was in terms of leading the country to its freedom and total independence. He would have seen the selfishness and the ignorance of his sons and the wickedness in the hearts of his heirs, and what they are doing to his beloved country today. What would have made him bitter is the sabotage of the sovereignty of the country advocated by his heirs. He would have been so outraged to hear their argument concerning the suspension of the country's constitution that, he would surely have cursed them out **"ONICOBY,"** in his dialect, because when he was alive, he could barely put up with such behavior of ignorance.

The ladder of evolution:

HOUPHOUET BOIGNY WAS A WISE MAN. He knew that after the era of slavery, colonialism would take over, and after that, we would get our freedom by fighting for it. He was conscious of the following events:

- From a point in time to the 60's, was the time of slavery in full force.

- From the 60's to the year 2000 was the time of colonialism covered up, and a modernized version of servitude; the accords of cooperation.

- From 2000 and above would be the time to break loose from the colonizers in order to build true partnerships with other countries. We would be relying first on our resources in Africa, then exchange technologies with the industrial world to develop our countries and our continent.

Houphouët Boigny was aware of that, but at the same time, he knew that we would encounter opposition from the oppressors during (the battle without), and hindrance from our own brothers who would not understand the scope of our battle, and this will constitute the purpose of (the battle within). I am utterly persuaded that our brothers know the purpose of our battle, but they chose to collaborate with the oppressors. This is so simple that you don't need a college degree to understand that we need to act collectively in order to claim liberty from our oppressors; for Jesus said: "**A kingdom that is divided against itself never prospers.**"

The African people are divided even within their own homes, regions, and countries, so it makes things difficult for those who have the right vision to succeed.
That is why the oppressor always thinks that he can continue to advocate his colonial influence on the small and feeble countries in the continent.

- You don't need your subject and your verb to agree to understand that strength comes from Unity, and that all God's creations (human and animals) need freedom at one point during their existence.

- You don't need to know about Plato and Aristotle to understand that it is our responsibility as a people to create our own environment of freedom.

- You don't need to know the theory of relativity to understand that the oppressor will not grant us freedom, or change the laws to set us free if we don't stand up on our feet to not only express it boldly, but to grapple to the commitment, and not lurk, until we acquire our total freedom. You don't need to know the second theory of thermodynamics in physics to understand that it is time to claim our freedom as a people.

All we need is to take our destiny in our own hands and take actions towards our freedom. We can not do it alone as human, so we need to seek the knowledge of our father God, and our Lord and Savior Jesus Christ who is the light, the truth, and the gateway to life, and then we will set ourselves in a position to understand that time has evolved.

So much is at stake that we can no longer tolerate to dwell under the rule and the clutches of a colonizer from whom we must obtain permission to develop our countries. We can no longer tolerate to obtain permission for the simplest things such as purchasing a vehicle from China or elsewhere, as a country. And why should these vehicles we purchase abroad have to transit in France for overhead fees added to the original cost? Or why having French contractors as absolute choice to build a bridge, and being forbidden to bargain and pick a contractor from another country who may offer a reasonable and cheaper price. For instance for a project that may cost $1 million if done by a contractor from another country, we may end up paying $ 10 million (ten times) the cost of the same job if done by a French contractor. This practice has been going on since the beginning of time. It is one of the clauses contained in the colonial contracts, now called accords of cooperation, **which we need to combat today**. We Africans are all held accountable for our actions concerning the welfare of our countries and our continent. We have to consider our ways before we can blame Chirac for his part of responsibility. We need to acknowledge that we, the African people are the problems of our continent. Many are those who commit mistakes and errors, and blame others for them instead of taking responsibility, and taking corrective measures.

All the associates of G7 who are accusing President Gbagbo of being the obstacle of their peace process have forgotten that we are in this predicament today because they organized a coup d'état that failed, then turned it into a rebellion. In other word, the root cause of the peace process is the failed coup d'état and the rebellion. Instead of facing it, taking their courage in two hands, and frantically admitting that:
"Behold, we have failed and it looks like we will never succeed.
Therefore let us give up our idea of overthrowing
President Gbagbo, and let us revise our positions, meet our

brothers and sisters half way, and start anew with a different attitude so we can normalize things and have the Presidential election as mature people," they are holding on to the rebellion and their treacherous peace process. All they have achieved is to hold us back for fifty years. .

LET US ADMIT THAT, Côte d'Ivoire was at peace until Alassane Dramane Ouattara came on board. Here is a man who is running after the power by all means necessary, and who has no other way of getting it than organizing coups d'état in this new millennium. He still does not know that time has evolved, and that the era of coups d'état is obsolete. He has never been incriminated, and he never will, so he thinks he is clean. He still goes around discrediting President Laurent Gbagbo, and Côte d'Ivoire; and haranguing, as usual that "I will be the President of Côte d'Ivoire," without stating how; by the way we know; and also, dreams are permitted.

Former President Bédié, the promoter of the term **"Ivoirité"** knew that he did not have the wit to resolve this issue, and left it hanging to the point where he literally messed up the country. He created such a spirit of ethnical division, and a state of tribalism as we had never seen before. He led the country almost to the point of a civil war. As a result of his negligent and sloppy leadership, the country succumbed in a near chaos, where people of the opposition parties resented people of his party, and even families begun to break up for political reasons, when husbands and wives did not share the same views.
Instead of feeling sorry, he has the nerve to accuse others. He has never been incriminated and he never will. He also thinks that he is not the problem of Côte d'Ivoire.

Soro Guillaume the chief rebel who is holding the Northern part of the country hostage is the hero to many, and to all our enemies. He is the new rich man growing; enjoying life and honors. He will never be incriminated. He even has the nerves to blame other people, after committing all these crimes, some of which we will never hear about.

If all the above mentioned individuals are innocent, who then is the blame for the problems of Côte d'Ivoire? While you are reading this page, ask yourself the following question:

"The country raised me, fed me, instructed me, and gave me the best that a mother can possibly give to her child. Now that I am grown and I should give back to her, where do I stand? How am I acting towards her? Do I feel that I have the right to kill her innocent babies, children, women and men who have nothing to do with politics?"

Remember, when out of jealousy, Cain killed his brother Abel, God called him and asked him: "Cain, where is your brother Abel?" And he answered God sarcastically saying; "am I Abel's keeper?" And God cursed him. All of you, enemies of Côte d'Ivoire, killers of the countries' babies, and the disturbers of the peace in the country, God will surely deal with you and reward you according to the work of your hands.

I am saying this because I am only human with feelings and emotions. Though I believe that there will come a time when the opportunity will be given to those killers to repent so that our merciful God can forgive them. The families of the victims will have no choice but to forget and do according to the recommendations of God as well. There is hope, I believe that we will all come together again as a nation, and we will be able to travel freely from the South to the North; from the East to the West, back and forth without the fear of a heartless rebel, or the danger of being killed. I believe that the unification of our country is possible by the **GRACE** of **GOD** who has the mighty power of **TRANSFIGURATION**. He will touch the rebels and murderers, and turn their lives around, as he did to Saul who later became Paul the apostle. All these murderers will become servants of the **ALMIGHTY GOD**, and the **LORD JESUS CHRIST**. Their knees shall bow and their tongues shall confess that **JESUS is the Lord**. This will be the time for them to freely burn their guns, and break ties with their sponsor Chirac, the destroyer of the African countries. They will be delivered and become normal people again. I will not be surprised to see Soro Guillaume preaching the **Word of God**, and evangelizing. I will not be afraid to approach him and listen to him preach. Then the Houphouëtists will realize that they were wrong since the beginning, and break their demonic alliances, and reconsider their ways. This will be the right time for them to come to their senses and realize that their father: Houphouët Boigny did not leave them such a legacy because he was a prince of peace, and not a prince of hatred and ignorance.

Ref: **Deuteronomy 4: 1-6** says,

"For he is coming to consider every man's work, whether good or evil…" The people who promised that they will render Côte d'Ivoire ungovernable, and they did, will have their reward. Only satan and his agents work everyday to make life a living hell for the children of God. Even though they know they have limited power to do so, they still try. So by saying what you said above, tell me if you are different from satan. I challenge you today and I inform you that you are defeated in the name of **Jesus Christ**. You have no power to render this country chaotic, and ungovernable. Our Merciful **God** will clean the country up out of your dirt and filth, and remake it a safer place to live; He will make it governable in the name of **Jesus Christ**.

Chapter Eleven:
Colonialism, Rebellion, The logistics of the rebellion
The spirit of rebellion, and Ignorance

COLONIALISM IS A MAN-MADE SET OF LAWS, or a method that a nation advocates on a certain country or people. It is the control or governing influence of a nation over dependent countries, territories or people.

It is the system or policy by which a nation maintains or advocates such influence or control. It is the state or the condition of being colonial or oppressed. This is not something that the oppressed nation gets out of, waiting for the oppressor to change the laws.

Colonialism is the barricades that have kept the African countries subjected, and in poverty with their resources, and the continent from developing itself.
It is the new form of slavery (neo-colonialism) that places the oppressed countries or continent in a condition of inferiority. Colonialism is a condition of deprivation of liberty, justice, and independence. It is a condition that places the oppressed countries in a state of servitude, and exploitation; and it takes away all rights of representation.

There is only one way to get out of this man made condition, just like segregation in South America where, on the buses as well as in public places, black people were kept in the back rows in a state of inferiority; and apartheid in South Africa. These inhuman conditions were practiced until one day, a small spark of freedom lit up among blacks in America, and in South Africa. One thing to notice is that these Europeans did not voluntarily change the conditions of the black people. They stood up for themselves to express the need for their freedom. The battle was fierce, yet deadly, but it was worth fighting. As a result today, this change in condition is celebrated in America as **Dr. Martin Luther King day**. Also South Africa has shaken off apartheid through the lengthy and painful struggle of **Honorable Nelson Mandela**, and his peers of the ANC.

That is why I am calling upon all the African people, young, and old, especially people from the French colonies; whether they live in the continent or overseas, to stand up and do something for themselves. They have to seize the situation of Côte d'Ivoire as an opportunity, an argument and a precedent to tell Chirac and others that enough is enough; that we can no longer take this Bs. What happened in Côte d'Ivoire happened for a purpose. Therefore the President of Côte d'Ivoire should not have to struggle alone against the oppressors. This is a collective cause, so the battle should be fought collectively, instead of some playing the hypocrites, while they are having hard times in their own countries. It is time to reverse things in a way to uplift the living conditions of our populations, and mold the image of our continent. Unfortunately, many do not see it this way. I would like to reiterate this to the African people; **no one will develop your countries, or change the social and economic conditions of your continent for you. So if you do not think of creating jobs for the youths in your countries, do not expect Chirac to come and do this for you. If you do not build your roads, schools and hospitals, do not expect him to do those infrastructures for you. It is your sole responsibility. Therefore, stop wasting time talking, but start acting**.

The generation of Dr. Kwamé Nkrumah, Patrice Lumumba and their peers fought to claim liberty of the African people. Their cause was just and noble, but they had no weapons and no armies to back them up, so they were crushed. The next generation of Presidents that took over could not continue to fight because they were tied up. They were more about building self-images, rather than changing the condition of Africa. For forty years or more they were caught up between debts, civil wars and genocides, unconsciously smudging the image of the continent.

The second phase of the battle has just begun with the rising of President Laurent Gbagbo in power. Unfortunately, in the West he is alone against the oppressors. He has no one to back him up except the youths; the patriots who are enduring the sufferings and the aftermath of the rage of the former colonizer, and the few children of God who understand that there is a time for bondage, and a time to cross the desert. You can see that those who call themselves the politicians are on a different route as if we were not in the same country. They are deaf, unable to hear the screaming, and feel the pain of the young people. They have no clue about patriotism either. God made it clear to us so that we would not make excuses that we were not aware of the choices we had to make. He said: **"I have set before you Life and death, but I encourage you to choose Life so that you and your children may live."**

While the neighbors have chosen to keep their countries under oppression, by playing the game of Chirac the colonizer, we, the Ivorian people, have chosen to get out of colonialism regardless of the intimidation of Chirac, and the price that comes along with it.
LIFE IS BASED ON CHOICES.

Rebellion:

REBELLION IS THE SEED that produces the tree of death, calamities, tragedies and desolation. It is the main technology of

France in all the French colonies.

Rebellion is the work of satan, the chief rebel. His purpose is to kill, steal, and destroy. Rebels take weapons to do just that; the work of their father. He comes to make orphans, crippled for life; physically and emotionally.

Rebellion creates poverty, misery, hunger - farmers who eke out a living can no longer work on their farms for fear to be killed by rebels.

Rebellion has caused so much desolation to the continent of Africa; you name Uganda, Rwanda, Somalia, Ethiopia, Liberia, Niger, Angola and Sierra Leone, and now Côte d'Ivoire. Just to name these few countries. It is the system by which the looters of the continent have economically weakened Africa, and they have succeeded to vacuum the resources of our countries. Until we unite as a people and realize our shortcoming, and find a cure for it, Africa will remain where it is; "the only third world continent."

There is a picture that I can never take out of my mind, as much as I try to erase it. I was in my hotel room in Antwerp, in Belgium one night on October 23, 2004. As I was watching television, a show came on about Sierra Leone. I took interest in the show at first because it talked about diamonds, until they showed a woman braiding the hair of a 4 year old girl whose two arms were cut off. When I saw this girl, I started to cry like a child. I began to reflect, and thought about my own baby girl who had just turned one; seeing myself raising my baby with her arms cut off by some rebels. What kind of sense would I ever make out of this, trying to explain what happened to her when she grows up and asked me? "Daddy, I see my friends with their arms, why mine are not there? What happened to me?" I cried so much that I fell sick as a result.

My every day prayer to God is to keep me alive so I can raise my children to maturity. Our life as human begins to have a real meaning when we start knowing our father God, creator of all things, and then we start taking responsibilities towards our children. But rebellion takes it away, violating and corrupting our rights of parenthood.

The next day when I woke up and I thought about that little girl that I saw on TV the previous night, I started to think about what might have happened to her in reality during that very doom hour. Knowing that rebels do not have sense, and a human heart, I am sure they killed the father, the mother and all the siblings, leaving the little girl alone. They probably molested her continually, torturing her and mocking her, and then they cut off her two arms for fun. She bled to death, feeling hungry, having no one to tend to her for hours, maybe days, before a surviving aunt found her half-dead. So much unspeakable tragedies have been inflicted to the children of Africa. I saw the video on the genocide in Rwanda. I could not believe what my eyes saw; miles and miles of human bodies lying on top of each other; bodies of babies who could barely speak, let alone knowing about politics; men and women slain as if they were not created by God, in His image. After the atrocities and the savagery committed by the rebels in Côte d'Ivoire, I heard some chilling testimonies. Those surviving victims who testified during the reconciliation period were selected. Obviously, there are cases far worst than the testimonies we heard; cases that we will never hear about.

An eleven year old boy testifies:
"They killed my mother; they killed my father and my sisters. But they did not kill me and my little brother who was five years old. They told me to carry my brother on my back and run with him. They said if I don't do that, they will also kill me. So I put my brother on my back and started to run. Then I fell because I was tired. They forced me again to start all over. I was crying, and I was tired. Then they killed my brother and they left," he said.
Can you imagine what an eleven years old boy went through? He saw his father, mother and siblings killed before his eyes. He is left psychologically crippled for life. There will never be a total recovery for that child.

A woman was taken hostage and ill treated by rebels.
"They raped me. They were many. They abused me, and after they finished, they took the gun and put it in my vagina, and in my behind. They hurt me. I am no longer a woman; I am no longer a woman," and she burst in tears. **Another young woman tells her encounter with her husband and the rebels, while attempting to run away:**

"My husband and I ran in the forest as they came in the village and started to kill the villagers. I was hit with a machete, but I was able to escape with my husband. As we ran, we met another group of rebels. They caught my husband. I thought they were going to kill him, but they did not kill him. They cut his two heels off, and they left him crippled in a pool of blood. After they left the scene, I came back and found him, but he could not move. He told me that he was hungry. I ran in the forest for almost five miles and I found ripe papayas in one plantation. I collected them and brought them to him. He ate and told me to go, because if they come back and see me, they would kill me. I did not want to go and leave him alone, but he begged me, and I finally left because we heard them coming. So I left my husband alone, wounded and helpless in the forest. I know he is dead by now from bleeding, or they simply finished him."

The rebels in Côte d'Ivoire committed so much heinous crimes. Entire families have been wiped out as if they never existed. On their evil spree, the rebels set up road blocks as traps, and waited in the nearby woods to stop people. Any person who accidentally showed up became a victim. I was told that these practices are still going on. Now they call them [**the road cutters**.]

One escapee tells of these kinds of practices.
"We were five people: a pregnant woman and her husband, and my sister and my cousin, we were running away from the village that had just been attacked by a group of rebels. We were stopped by the rebels at the road block. The rebels started to harass us. They asked the pregnant woman about the sex of her baby. As she said

she did not know, one of the rebels said: "I am sure it is a boy." Another one said: "No, I know it is a girl," and they started to argue and bet on the sex of the infant. Then one of them pulled her on the side, and her husband yelled:

"Leave my wife alone,"

"Ok, she is your wife?" one rebel said, then added.

"Show us how you did it to get her that big. Take off your clothes and show us," he ordered, but the man resisted. The rebels tied him up, cut his sexual organ (pennies) off, and inserted it in his mouth. Then, to solve the issue, one of them slashed her belly with a machete, and opened her and took the baby out. "Hey! It is a boy," the rebels screamed joyfully. The man on the other side was bathing in a pool of blood, the woman as well. My sister fell on the ground and died just by seeing the cruelties.

My cousin and I got the courage to run away. They chased us, and they caught my cousin. I could hear her scream as they hit her probably with a machete. I was fortunate to escape. I don't know what has happened to her ever since.

One man testifies how the rebels attacked a village:

"In a neighboring village, as the rebels arrived, people ran for their lives. Some simply shut their doors and buried themselves under their beds. One woman had just given birth. Her husband and two children who went on their farm in the morning that day, met the rebels, and never returned home. Her mother advised her to stay indoors. She obeyed that day, but how long could she stay indoors without desiring to get out, to fetch water for her and the baby? A week later when she did, she was recuperated by the rebels. And when she pleaded that she had just given birth, that she was not feeling well, that she needed some water for the baby for her to take a bath, one of the rebels said to her: "You just had a baby? That is good; you can have a second one today." The rebels raped her repeatedly for several days. "Her mother did not know her whereabouts. Instead of letting her go to take care of her new born, the rebels killed her after they got tired of raping her."

Many unspeakable crimes and atrocities took place in the

Western and North Western parts of Côte d'Ivoire during the rebellion, more than anywhere else in the country. The Northerners who cheered then suffered as well.

My spiritual mother who is from Diouzon, in the region of Duékoué, was in tears when she was relating her story to me during her visit to Washington on January 10th, 2006.

"My son, a mouth can not speak what really took place. We can try to tell what we can, but what our people went through in reality is beyond belief. As the rebels entered Diouzon, it was 3.00 AM. This is their favorite time because they want to catch as many people as they can in their sleep, so they won't spare one soul. They began to pour kerosene on the houses and set them on fire while the people were asleep. Those who smelt the smoke and woke up to get out were shot at the doors. Only a few escaped from the village only to get caught before they even reached Duékoué. Among them were members of m*y family who tried to escape through the bush. They walked miles and miles during the night. Unfortunately, a few miles from Duékoué, they were caught by a group of rebels. They were twenty one people altogether, including my niece who was eight months pregnant, her eight years old son, her 5 years old daughter, and her mother who is my elder sister. In their rage, the rebels slaughtered them one by one, but when they reached my niece, they stopped and asked her;* "What is the sex of the baby in your womb?" As she said: "I don't know," *one of the rebels sliced her belly in two with a machete, and the baby fell on the ground. They shot the baby, and shot her. Then, they cut her and the baby, and asked her mother to cook the flesh for them. She refused and asked them to kill her as well. They took their time and cooked, then ate. They shot the little girl and her son and cut them also in pieces. They took the grand mother away for three months, using her as their wife. She was later released but she is no longer normal.*

The day she started to relate the encounter, she fell unconscious and we took her to the hospital where she stayed for two weeks before she regained consciousness. My village was burnt down. It does not exist any more.

As she spoke, she was in tears. I had neither the strength nor the courage to comfort her. I had pain in my heart as I listened religiously to her.

It seemed like a fairy tale, but it was nothing but the truth.

The logistics of the rebellion in Côte d'Ivoire:

THE REBELS IN CÔTE D'IVOIRE had two main targets during their killing spree:

1- The West, and

2- The Central West of Côte d'Ivoire.

1- The West was the region of the slain General Robert Guei. It was a target out of vengeance for eliminating Alassane Ouattara from the 2000 presidential race on the basis of his ambiguous nationality while the General was the head of the military transition. The General called him the multinational candidate. Bédié in his place of exile was probably blaming the General for his downfall, and sought vengeance by teaming up with Alassane, and Chirac.

2- The second target, the Central West, which is President Laurent Gbagbo's region. That region was a target because they feared that he might win the upcoming election because of his popularity, though they call him the minority President just to comfort themselves. But within them, they know the reality in the country. That is why they performed the killing of attrition in those areas to guarantee their success during the election.

Their goal was to slay as many people as they could in those two regions in order to make sure that the electoral vote there was reduced to the minimum, possibly eliminated to secure the victory of their candidate. What a wicked way of doing politics in Côte d'Ivoire, and in Africa?

THIS WAS THE LOGISTICAL ASPECT OF THE REBELLION.

The spirit of rebellion in general:

THE SPIRIT OF REBELLION operates the same way everywhere. In every country, the sufferings, the abuses, the harassments, and the killings are the same. The cruelties, the atrocities, and the hatred are the same everywhere in every country of the continent of Africa.

Life's attribute as set up by **God**, is the same for every human being; whether poor or rich; and pain that is inflicted upon our young ones is felt the same way by every human, whether rich or poor.

In neighboring Sierra Leone, I saw gruesome images that, if you are not strong enough, can cause you to have a heart attack. I was heartbroken looking in the eyes of babies and young children with hands and legs amputated by rebels; a mother with a bleeding hand, weeping over her baby with a bullet in the head; mothers with their breasts cut off purposely; fathers with their arms and legs cut off, and young girls raped, burned and killed. Seeing these photos, and reading in the eyes of the victims, my thoughts strayed, trying to reconstruct a portion of the horrid moment they endured.

As Rod Stewart sings; "Every picture tells a story," the story of these victims begins a little while before their lives were about to take another form, the kind they had never expected while going by their daily businesses in their villages around love ones.

Before that dreadful moment, daily life goes on with the routine of farm works and house chores. Usually these people endure tragic moments that are quickly dealt with by comforting each other. Though poverty is their heritage, the love for one another muffles their misfortune, and deadens their hardships. And these courageous farmers live happily with what their creator, and only hope in life God, has given them as substance. All seems peaceful, and nothing can surpass that moment of joy, chiefly when night falls, and they gather around the evening wine servers, bringing the last chapter of the day to a close.

They feel at home, and they have nothing to worry about. But suddenly, out of all expectations, it seems as if the peace in the village had been programmed by their own people who are supposed to protect them, to end, and turn their destiny upside down.

Suddenly, when gun shot are heard out of nowhere, interfering with the peace they had been enjoying for free, they have no time left to ask questions. And from that moment on, very swiftly, their lives seems to be connected with doom, and caught up with dread that takes them in a vicious and hellish swirling, like a fierce whirlwind that blows and uproots trees. And for an endless and indefinite period of time, they are mercilessly tortured. And later when it all fades away, and calm seems to set in, the survivors are left with new daily chores consisting of: coping with rotting dead bodies, stench that now fills the air, helping the amputees feed and move around, tending to one another's wounds, and learning to live in the desolation. They are left bereft of half of their lives; which leaves them with two questions without answer:

1- Why? 2- Did satan thirst for our blood? Or did he hunger for the flesh of our babies?

Ishmael Beah from Sierra Leone takes us on a long and aimless journey through the thick forest of Sierra Leone, as he tells his horrific encounter of the senseless war in his country. He braves death, loneliness, wild beasts, venomous snakes, and then rebels who hold him at gun point on various instances. He escapes miraculously all obstacles, hoping to reunite with his family one day. During his perilous journey, he comes across, acquaints, and then joins a group of escapee boys, and they carry on together. One day, he hears news about his family's whereabouts, which strengthens him. Many days of walk later, when he and his companions finally approach the village where his family had managed to find refuge, the thoughts of seeing his love ones again, perhaps in their entirety, overwhelms him with joy. **Unfortunately, his whole world was about to crumble forever.**

A couple of miles away from that distant village, and a step away from seeing his love ones, Ishmael and his friends meet a native who seems familiar to them, and reassures him with fresh news of his family. But soon after they decide to carry on after taking a moment of rest, doom interferes, and Ishmael's joy is shattered forever. They hear gun shots, and cries of pain and desperation echo from a distance. "What is happening?" they exclaim. A little while later, they see a thick layer of black smoke rising from the village. As they speed up to enter the village, all that remains of it is desolation. The whole village looks like hundreds of Bulldozers came in, steamrolling everything in their path. Animals strewn on the streets and alleys, motionless, and every house has been ransacked and set ablaze with its occupants trapped in it. "They lived here." When the villager points to Ishmael the house that once served as a sanctuary for his family, he rushes in amidst flames and thick smoke, only to find ashes as the remain of his love ones. His entire family had just perished. Ishmael Beah is left heartbroken, with only one question in his mouth: **WHY?**

Ignorance:

THE LORD SAYS in the book of **Hosea 4: 6**
"My people perish for lack of knowledge."
Lack of knowledge Implies ignorance; and knowledge comes from acquainting with the word of God.

REBELLION FEEDS on ignorance.

When he was eager to have our Lord **Jesus Christ** crucified, satan was ignorant of the purpose of God, not knowing that he was prompting his own downfall at the same time. Had he known that he was the main instrument for the fulfillment of the promise of God for humanity, he would have never ordered the crucifixion of the SON OF GOD. As much as he is ignorant, so are all the ungodly who work for him.

The devil has moved in our nations to utilize those who lack knowledge and do not fear God, as instruments of discord, misunderstanding, and confusion. They see the truth, they know it but they are pursuing the purpose of their father. Many are the African people who have the wrong concept of doing politics. They are power hungry, and going through the process of campaigning until the election takes place is too long a way for them. They ignore what running for power entails, so they choose the short cut. Today in this new millennium, they are still not ashamed to seek power through coups d'état.

Satan, their father has kept them in a state of ignorance, enabling them to overlook the truth, accusing the victims for being the obstacles of the so called peace process. They know very well that the problem lies on their side, but they are so selfish and self-centered that their only option is to stick to their lies, and continue to harass President Laurent Gbagbo. During the crisis, he yielded to most of their groundless requests. He even signed a decree, making exceptionally Alassane eligible for the next Presidential Elections, by referring to the article # 48 of the Ivorian constitution; one of the two articles Chirac and Kofi Annan said should not be referred to during the transition in their resolution # 1721. All these efforts did not suffice for the rebels to disarm as expected. The new request today is that the President has to leave office so they can control the country. What they could not obtain with weapons, they are thinking they will obtain it with resolutions and simple words of intimidation.

We are grateful today to have on our side: **The United States, China, Russia, Tanzania, and South Africa**. These countries understand the sovereignty of any country through its constitution. They believe in the freedom of any nation under the sky; whether it is a rich, poor, big or small country. This is something that Chirac and the Ivorian politicians ignore. They probably learned about it in school, but they are so haunted by the spirit of ignorance and the culture of under humanism that applying the common rule of sovereignty to their own country becomes a nightmare. It was not too long in 1993, when some of them enjoyed the privilege of the fundamental law that bestows the very sovereignty to the country, and took office. At that time if we opposed them by attempting to suspend the constitution to prevent its use, they would have fought us fiercely, or treated us as insane.

In 2006, the same individuals are rallying to have the same constitution suspended because someone else is in power. We find this hard to understand, and to believe. Only the spirit of ignorance can drive people to act the way the Ivorian politicians are behaving. They have visibly lost all senses of reasoning; though they claim they are intellectuals. It has not been a century when President Laurent Gbagbo granted the eligibility of Alassane Ouattara for the Presidential election by applying the article # 48 of the constitution. He is rallying to have the constitution trashed not knowing that he is nullifying his candidacy. This is the kind of ignorance that we have to deal with in Côte d'Ivoire, and the kind of audience that President Laurent Gbagbo is facing.

Honestly speaking, lines should be drawn, and guidelines should be set in life if we are to avoid living in a jungle like world. We should know better not to temper with some crucial elements we can not control, if we are to enjoy the virtues of creation. Even a man made computer comes in every household with firmware that the end user is prohibited to temper with, if he wants to enjoy its outputs. He is free to add, and remove any software he sees fit. Tempering with the firmware can damage the computer. The same theory goes with the air we breathe. We do not see it, and we do not control that mechanism. As a human being, if you try to temper with the flow of air in your lungs, you know you are a dead man.

A nation, although being a moral entity, has its attributes of life. Besides the territory, the population, and the government, the constitution is the common law that symbolizes its sovereignty. We can speculate or reason, act like fools, and say anything we want to say with no regard of others if we can get away with it, though all is not permitted to say. But we should spare the sovereignty of our countries, unless we agree that we have truly lost our minds. Just like putting up with someone tempering with your birth certificate. How would you feel? All written constitutions are not perfect at first; that is why the writers set aside a bill of rights called amendments for further improvements. This prevents the misuse of the constitution when an article does not apply any more. We have never seen in history, a country where a constitution was declared invalid, and then trashed. The Ivorian political scene is unique in the world, with the country's own children making alliances to trash its fundamental law; trying everything possible to make sure they render their own brother powerless; to achieve just that. The voice of President Laurent Gbagbo has echoed in a jungle like world where the weak is crushed, and the strong prevails. We have found ourselves in a land where bitterness and intolerance have grown roots to overshadow the love and the brotherliness which once characterized the Ivorian people. Hatred bodes to the extent that sons of the country have joined forces to destroy their nation without feeling the pain as if their brother was an intruder. We can only blame ignorance that has entered into the lives of the Ivorian people.

Praise the LORD, that all of us have not fallen under that spell. **Thanks to GOD** for giving Côte d'Ivoire and the Ivorian people a President, filled with an overwhelming desire and commitment to safeguard the sovereignty of the country, and to protect its interests from predators.

Côte d'Ivoire is proud to have him as President, and the youth (the patriots) as sons. What would Côte d'Ivoire have been if all of us were thinking, reasoning, and behaving likewise? Obviously, it would be a disaster.

The whole continent of Africa is undergoing a major crisis by our own fault. Many still believe that their salvation lies in the hands of the former colonizers. They still rely on coups d'état to take power, and the intimidation, the harassment and the killing of innocent people to get where they want to get. Thanks to God for the few who have crossed the boundary of ignorance to set themselves in the light. It is a shame to see intellectuals getting together to tear their country down. Right after failing to take power illegally, they claim elections as if President Gbagbo denied elections to the country. Instead of coming in grips with their shame and asking forgiveness for their misconduct, they want to teach us lessons. They are not willing to give up on their theory of harassment and intimidation, because they have put their trust in their master, and their guns.

But the **LORD** says in **PSAUMES 125**:

"They that trust in the **LORD** shall be as mount Zion, which cannot be removed, but abides forever.

2- As mountains are round about Jerusalem, so the **LORD** is round about his people from henceforth even forever.

3- For the rod of the wicked shall not rest upon the lot of the righteous; lest the righteous put forth their hands unto iniquity.

4- Do good, O **LORD**, unto those that be good, and to them that are upright in their hearts.

5- As for such as turn aside unto their crooked ways, the **LORD** shall lead them forth with the workers of iniquity: but peace shall be upon Israel."

Chapter Twelve:
God's creation / evil on the rise

HUMAN, **CREATED BY GOD IN HIS LIKENESS**, have the capacity of doing good to humanity. But sadly, though, there are many who have chosen to commit unspeakable acts of destruction, breaking away from the commands of God.

Evil on the rise

Why then humans are responsible for so much evil in the world? God did not create man to do evil. God created man in His image to love his neighbors, give free to the needy, worship God and replenish the earth. Man was to find his true identity and crave for the knowledge of God. The more man would know God, the more he would get close to Him and be inspired continually, and be inclined to do good; Just that, and back off from evil. This would be the fruit of knowledge. Sadly though, human who has turned away from his creator, God Almighty, shed more blood than he does good in the world. As a result of that, we see today that there is more hatred than love; more evil than good in the world. Whosoever adheres or agrees with evil doers, or sits in the same seat as them is also an evil doer, not only he who commits the evil acts.

In fact the chief rebel pulled Adam and Eve into rebelling against God in the garden where they dwelled. They in turn produced a human race with evil inclination. **Genesis 8:21.** Rebels and all who associate with them are doers of inequity, which in turn is the product of ignorance. The fruits thereof are mass murders, rapes, pillaging, etc, which are enemies of civilization.

In the republic of Congo (DRC) one of President Mobutu's practices was pillage. He randomly sent out his militia men to plunder, and loot the population. And these fools executed without identifying themselves as being part of the victims, and they took advantage of the situation and satisfied their lust by raping young girls, as well as married women at gun point, most of the time before the eyes of their husbands.

People grow up building up selfish desires, and these desires develop and produce sins, and these sins produce the fruits that we witness in the world today: rebellions, genocides, coups d'état, death of innocent people, and then desolation. The chief rebel in Côte d'Ivoire, Soro Guillaume wrote a book entitled;
"Why I became a rebel." I don't think there are more than two reasons why someone becomes a rebel. Either you become one, pursuing your father's work, or you are recruited to run an errand for someone.

"Why I became a rebel."
I did not read Mr. Soro's book to see the reasons he evoked. But one thing that I am certain of is that: Mr. Soro had no cause for which he was fighting. *When someone recruits you to run an errand consisting of overthrowing a government, and you get paid for the job*, it means that you do not have a cause.
Any person who has a cause always fights until the end of time. He does not settle for someone else's philosophy.
Therefore, the answer to Mr. Soro's above question is this:
"Because he was ignorant."

If we have honest people in Côte d'Ivoire, they will convene with us that we saw **ONE MAN** who fought consistently Houphouët Boigny. That man had a cause for which he was fighting. He vied for change in Côte d'Ivoire. Houphouët tried to thwart his cause on several occasions with huge sums of money, but this man faulted not. Instead, he fought fiercely, but intelligently, and non-violently until the day he took power through election as he has always claimed. This man is the actual President of Côte d'Ivoire, **his Excellency, President Laurent Gbagbo.**

A patriot would never act the way Soro Guillaume acted; being used to kill on behalf of someone else. Suppose we all took guns because each one of us had an issue, imagine what kind of country Côte d'Ivoire would have become. For sure our country would never be the positive reference it has always been; it would surely have been called: (*the country of "idiots" where people don't have mouths to express themselves. They use guns to even say good morning to their neighbors.*)

When Saul (who later became Paul the apostle) condoned, and participated in evil against early Christians, he proved in the book of **Acts 9: 5-6** that **"he was ignorant"** of the **LORD,** so he asked **"Who are you LORD?"** and **"What wilt thou have me to do?"** Paul acknowledged that when someone else uses you to run such a snarling errand, it means you are ignorant, or overwhelmed by an unclean spirit.

News for you:

JESUS says to all rebels and killers across the globe:
"You are from your father the devil, and you wish to do the desires of your father. He was manslaughter when he began." **John 8:44**

Remember; satan has no power to force people to do evil. This means, if you become a rebel, it is simply by choice; no one forced you to become one. Satan did not force you either. God commended you to choose life, and you did not, because you were ignorant. For your knowledge, JESUS is coming to crush the head of satan, and all the political systems, many of which are engaged in killing, and advocate genocides, rebellion, colonialism, and servitude throughout the world. **Ecclesiastic 4: 1- 9** To all of you who have become the rebels in Africa, and are taking pleasure in shedding the blood of your brothers and sisters; the lives of the children you have killed will remain a burden over your heads for a long time. The orphans, the widows and cripples you have produced will live with the trauma for a long time as well, unless if you can promise to bring their [*love ones*] back to life; which is virtually impossible. It is easy to blame others for your fate, or find excuses to justify your crimes, or reasons to substantiate your malevolence; howbeit, one thing is plausible; you the killers will never find a remedy to mend the broken hearts. Tell me; where is your spirit of brotherhood? Where is your sense of **GOD**'s commandment that stipulates: "love thy neighbors as you love thyself." How then can you slaughter your neighbor and claim you love yourself?

He, who has an ear, let him hear.

Chapter Thirteen:
The generation of victims

AFRICA, ALTHOUGH VERY RICH in human, as well as natural and mineral resources, is still stuck in the mud of the "**Third World**" perimeter; whereas many of her teammates, not to say all, have shaken off the mud, and are now occupying a seat around the table of the Super Powers.

Being marginalized and identified as a group member, and stereotyped with a disparaging name according to a particular condition, at a certain time in life, should not be upsetting. But the earlier aversion that one raises out of this calling, and the kinds of initiatives one takes afterwards in order to remain, or to pull out of that degrading condition or state, is the problem.

Brazil is no longer part of the third world. The villages of old have been transformed into cities, and many programs and opportunities have been created there. China, Japan, and others have long gone by taking drastic initiatives and making changes. For instance around the 1950's, Asian children were sent abroad: in the United States, England, and Europe, to study.
These children were called back later into their respective countries, and the old men favored their insertion into the various sectors of the economy, and society, and allowed them to apply the skills and knowledge they acquired abroad. The old men were all in a communion of spirit in such a way that all obstacles of

jealousy, sorcery, witchcraft and threats of death, all the fruits of the power of darkness that hinder development were taken out of their system and society. Bureaucracy which is another factor of hindrance in the development process was also eliminated. President Mao Se Tung decreed that all sleeves be folded, and everybody should go to work, and it was done in a harmonious and collaborative spirit. They did not rely on a colonizer, but on their own children whom they sent abroad and came back home. They did not outsource either. Everything was done by their children. For example at one moment when there was no more land fields to cultivate rice, a group of young experts introduced a system whereby the roof tops of certain buildings were used as land fields to cultivate rice. China became the world leader of rice production, and it still is.

In the case of Africa, things are different.

First of all African governments select people of their choice, and send them to specific training school abroad according to what they have assessed as their needs, leaving out the real needs of the countries. Secondly, the same old people who started politics in the 1950s or before are still holding on tight. They even get jealous when the young men arrive from abroad with their skills, and degrees to suggest innovative ways in terms of contributing to the development of their countries. These old men get so offended that they represent a threat to the young men. They think that these skilled young men came to compete with them instead of looking at it as an opportunity; so they assume;
"They have come to take our places."

Africa is run on old thoughts, expired ideas, and out dated systems. The old building of the African system needs to be demolished, and reconstructed with steal and fresh walls, so to speak. We need to **cut**, **destroy**, and **uproot**, then start **building** a total new image and a new system in the continent of Africa.

I had the privilege to talk to many talented and skilled brothers and sisters from Africa, who studied abroad. After we had

a short conversation about the disquieting condition of the continent, they have virtually the same reactions:
"I went once to try to help them in a particular area according to my credentials, but I almost got killed. By God's Grace, I was able to make it back here unscathed; I will never go back again to try to help them; they don't need help." All the African brothers and sisters that I met and talked to, regardless of their country of nationality feel the same way about how the continent is ran. *"If these old people are still competing against us, when will we have the opportunity to come on board and contribute to the development of our countries and our continent?"* many said to me.

Africa today needs new and fresh ideas, and a new spirit to get out from where she is, for **JESUS** says:
"You cannot pour new wine in old bottles. Or sow a new fabric over an old one." This is so true because you will not get a lasting result when you do the above things. This is exactly why God did not allow the children of Israel to enter the promise land for the first time. Moses sent spies into the land God promised to give them, to search it out and bring a report in order to determine the best way to go in and possess the land. The spies came back from their mission, but the report was not inspiring.
"Yes, is it a good land that the Lord our God has given us; notwithstanding, we shall not go in because the people is greater and taller than we; the cities are great and walled up to heaven; and moreover we have seen the sons of the Anakims there," the spies reported at their arrival.
But Caleb and Joshua disagreed with them and said:
"We know we saw the sons of the Anakims, but we can go in and possess the land. Our God who brought us out of Egypt, and fought for us all these nations which we conquered, will go before us and fight our enemies for us," said Caleb and Joshua.

The children of Israel wanted to go back to Egypt. This means that they were not ready to renew their thoughts in order to enter the promise land. You can not enter your prophetic destiny with your old mentality and ideas. So God asked them to go back into the desert. He said to them:

"Surely there shall not one of these men of this generation see that good land which I promised to give to your fathers, except Caleb, the son of Jephunneh, and Joshua the son of Nun shall see it. Moreover your children, which in that day had no knowledge between good and evil, unto them will I give it, and they shall possess it."

When you stick to your old thoughts and you refuse to renew them and take initiatives, you can never get out of your initial condition and prosper. That is why God gave us the mind to think constantly in order to innovate. This should be our time to work for our countries and our continent; unfortunately we are confronted with obstacles of all kinds: conflicts of interests, hatred, jealousy, greed, selfishness and so on. There are no opportunities for us in our own land. That is why many risk their lives everyday on boats and canoes, fleeing to Europe in search for a better life. Unfortunately many get caught up in storms at sea, and just perish in the process of running away from misery at home. The idea of taking action to combat poverty muffles the severity of the sufferings of family members. Their souls will be at peace knowing that they died trying to accomplish a goal, even though loved ones will undergo double portion of pain. The African leaders are not embarrassed and ashamed by this. They act as if everything was normal. They attend meetings abroad with leaders of developed countries, making promises they never keep, and they do not care about how people in the developed world see them and feel about them. The thing that baffles me is the daily busy schedules our leaders assign themselves to, making them virtually inaccessible. Fine, but twenty or thirty years later you see the same dirty roads severely eroded away with holes like on mine fields, and the old infrastructures the white people left forty years ago, unimproved, never maintained, or merely crumbling under the weight of ruin, etc. And you ask yourself; "what were they busy doing for the past thirty or forty years?"

I have never seen people who love power so much anywhere else than in Africa; they would do anything to cling to it even on the brink of death. You think, perhaps they have the best interests of the countries at heart; instead, they are acting conspicuously numb to the outcry of hungry children, living next door to them in complete squalor – blind to the deterioration of living conditions, and the debacle of the economy – or totally ascetic, with no political ax to grind; passing expedient laws to instill fear and dread in the atmosphere, while securing their power for life. And you wonder; when will sanity ever prevail here? Because of that, we have been forced to become the **generation of victims, and losers** coping with the scourge of African dictators and warlords. Even with our knowledge, skills, talents, and our overwhelming desire to contribute to the development of our countries and our continent, we are snubbed by our own people. Nevertheless, we can reverse the equation by taking the right kinds of actions. There is hope, I believe, but we need to wake up and act collectively, and positively.

Chapter Fourteen:
Xenophobia

I WAS TEMPORARILY FLUMMOXED WHEN I HEARD THE WORD "**XENOPHOBIA,**" being ascribed to Côte d'Ivoire. I literally took this as an affront, at first, then promptly after, emboldened myself to rise above the matter, telling myself: "*We have seen and heard worse than that. From the beginning of the crisis, we have been increasingly inured to the persistent torments of our adversaries. So there is no need now to grow restive over something minor such as this, and allow [yourself] to lose focus, when you have a calling.*"

God asked Moses:

"What do you have in your hand?" at the red sea bank. "Use what you have in your hand and speak to the sea," God said to him as he was being distracted by the crowd. So I was inspired outright by the Holy One, to use the talent and gift of letters he gave me, and I took a pen and pad to explain to the distorters what this word means and whether it applies to Côte d'Ivoire, my beloved country.

Xenophobia means:

Fear and hatred of strangers or foreigners or anything that is strange or foreign in nature.

A **xenophobe** person is:

Someone who is unduly fearful of what is foreign and especially of foreign origin.

This is the meaning of the word xenophobe, and xenophobia which have been unjustly ascribed to the Ivorian people, and to Côte d'Ivoire, in simple terms.

The only time the word xenophobe can be used is when people deliberately show hatred towards foreigners in a country. This word is never used in the event that citizens of a country are fussing over an issue. So let us assume that Alassane Ouattara is an Ivorian in conflict with his fellow Ivorian people; we can not refer to the word **xenophobia** in that case. We could genuinely refer to **"an internal conflict,"** instead of "xenophobia". Those who call us xenophobe are conscious that Alassane is not an Ivorian, but a foreigner. When Houphouët Boigny appointed him as his Prime Minister, the Ivorian people did not reject him for the respect of the old man. Why then are we called xenophobe?

I suggest that foreigners, including Alassane should know their place, and refrain from getting involved in the political life of our country. This goes with every country in the world. So foreigners in Côte d'Ivoire should leave politics to the Ivorian people. They have been living in the country for decades and have never encountered any disturbance until Alassane came and raised the wrong issue of being rejected based on his "Muslim" status.

When former President Henry Konan Bédié invented the term "Ivoirité," what he meant was: in order to run for the Presidency in Côte d'Ivoire, the candidate has to be an Ivorian born of a father and mother both Ivorian. This is not new to the world. I don't think that an Ivorian naturalized as a French citizen can seek Presidency in France. Regardless of his new status, he will not be permitted by the law.
So let us admit that; Côte d'Ivoire has never had a religious issue; thanks to God, such as Christians and Muslims in conflicts. The problem we are having now is that Alassane is using his Muslim status as a political topic. He said:
"They do not like me because I am a Muslim, and I come from the North." He has literally built his party on his religion.
Any political party built on religion should merely be

Two battles to win

dismantled and banned from activity. If we want to be stable in our fragile countries, let us pass fair and decent laws and enforce them to guarantee peace. Alassane knows the seriousness of this issue. He knows what he intended to achieve by raising such an issue. Also by saying the following: "**I will render this country ungovernable**," he knew the right formula to create a civil war. He wanted to stir a conflict between the peaceful Muslims and the Christians in Côte d'Ivoire, and have France come in to install him as President, on the ground that he is the only person capable of solving this issue; even though the same created it, they would not mention it. We all know that religious related issues are a source of endless conflicts around the world. We should know better by now not to engage on such a route. Alassane Ouattara is wrong by making the peaceful Muslim people in the country his sole audience, feeding them with the wrong information.
This is wrong altogether.

Every African country has its citizens in Côte d'Ivoire, and these foreigners are well rooted in the economic life of the country. When we consider things on a nationality level, we can see that all the sectors of our economy are divided among the foreigners. The Ivorian nationals are lost or non existent in the Ivorian economy, for example:
The Burkinabés and the Malians are holding the transportation monopoly, as well as the agricultural sector.
The Mauritanians have most of the grocery stores in Côte d'Ivoire. **The Lebanese** own the market of electronics, the supermarkets, and now the housing department.
The fish market at the sea port is in the hands of **the Nigerians.** The People from **Niger** have the market of coffee and the breakfast kiosks (Garba) that the youths crave. **The French** have most of the industries.
The Senegalese have the market of textile, and woodcraft; and the list goes on and on.

Due to their hospitality, the Ivorian people today are held hostage in their own country. They are well aware of that situation, but they never complained about it until Alassane came, raising a very dangerous issue. The total population of Côte d'Ivoire is approximately 18 million inhabitants comprising about 60 different dialects and ethnic groups. These ethnic groups are divided in seven large tribes, each corresponding to a percentage, in addition to a group of foreigners. In the chart below, you will see that the percentage of the group of foreigners (**27%**) is larger than the percentages of any of the large tribes (Akan **20%**, Mande **17%**, and Krou **12%**). With such a large number of foreigners in Côte d'Ivoire, how could such a country be tarred with xenophobia? This was a publicity of French Newspapers in the attempt to discredit us because their President could not obtain what he was after. They even found defect in the Ivorian coffee and cocoa; the very coffee that is labeled "**French coffee**" in all the supermarkets around the world. Not only that they found our products defective, but they accused us of using children as labor force on our cocoa and coffee fields. Very strange; no such a thing is taking place in Côte d'Ivoire. Our labor force is composed of adult foreigners. Chirac wanted to hurt Côte d'Ivoire by enticing the world buyers to snub the Ivorian products. This hateful behavior of Chirac towards Côte d'Ivoire depicted that he was restive after failing to achieve his goal. He was angry after spending a lot of money to cater to the rebellion without success.

Côte d'Ivoire: A Country Study

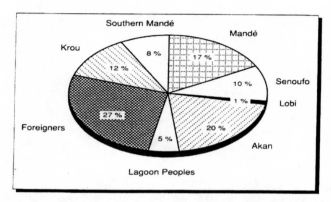

Source: Based on information from United States, Department of State, "The Tribes of the Ivory Coast," April 1970; and Côte d'Ivoire, National Census Information, 1976.

Figure 7. Percentage of Population by Ethnic Cluster, 1988

Chapter Fifteen:
Two nations in one

THE WAR OR THE CRISIS IN COTE D'IVOIRE IS a replica of the confrontation of the children of **God** against the Philistines with goliath at the front line, threatening the children of **God** for forty days and nights. That must have been very annoying. Remember young David, with one stone hit goliath at the forehead and killed him. The Philistines then fled.

Our enemies might be a legion when you look at the whole picture with your physical eyes. You can see that the rebels are in the North holding half of the country hostage; the opposition parties are in the country harassing the President, and Chirac in France is controlling the whole scenario, pressing the UN Security Council to suspend the Ivorian constitution. The children of **God** are then caught between them, having nowhere to turn, but our Lord is in control. This is why I encourage the Ivorian people, the children of the Most high to be strong in the Lord and not to be afraid of them because they are nothing. Keep your composure and pray endlessly as you have always done to your father who detains all powers.

The **Bible** says that when the **Lord** is with you, who can be against you? Who can defeat you when the **Lord** is your Shield? You may not have any sophisticated weapons to defend yourself, but remember that the wall of Jericho was not destroyed with demolishing machines. It fell at the sounds of trumpets and shouts.

Reminisce also how Gideon and his three hundred men delivered the children of Israel from the hands of the Medianites and the children of the East. With three hundred men against a legion of thieves, Israel was delivered at the sounds of trumpets.

Let me reveal to you today the reason why the French marines at the Hotel Ivoire shot at the Patriots. There are two things about the French soldiers. **1-** They are on high substances, and **2-** Most of them are spiritualists. **God** opened their eyes so he could show them the real danger that surrounded them; and when he did so, they were able to see the army of **God** on white horses and chariots, with burning swords in their hands. At that point, they felt threatened and tried to defend themselves against an army that was not physical, but they thought is was, so they started shooting. Later when it was all over, they realized they had shot at young people with bare hands. So they felt embarrassed, ashamed, and disoriented, therefore simply fled the scene. So, children of **God** in Côte d'Ivoire, this is your call. Do not be afraid. The restoration of your country is in your hands. It is your duty to defend it while selfish and ignorant politicians are destroying it.

The two spiritual kingdoms that constitute life have been identified in Côte d'Ivoire: **1- The Kingdom of God**, and the kingdom of satan. When a person belongs to the **Kingdom of God**, people will know it by the fruits that the person bears. Or, if the person belongs to the kingdom of satan, it will incontestably show as well by the fruits the person bears; no questions about it.

Chapter Sixteen:
Danger looms

NO ONE CAN DENY TODAY the fact that President Laurent GBAGBO, President of the FPI at that time, did warn the Ivorian people when he sensed trouble coming through his tinted binoculars of a well versed politician.

He warned loudly that the man, who had just been nominated as Prime Minister by President Felix Houphouët Boigny, was a Wolf in a Lamb's suit, and a big trouble for the country today, and the cause of an endless conflict for the generations to come. But no one seemed to pay him heed.

Those who are true to themselves can notice all the troubles the country went through since the dissonant nomination of Alassane Ouattara as Prime Minister. The Ivorian people thought they were ever exempt from coups d'état and rebellion. Many thought it could only happen to neighbors. They took peace for granted, and overlooked the danger Houphouët Boigny brought in the country, and later left us as a heritage. The truth is, regardless of what mistakes Houphouët might have made and left behind, our country could be spared all this trouble if we did not have selfish and self-centered politicians in the country. Because of their ignorance, they have led the country astray, after several early warnings from President Laurent Gbagbo. He saw the danger lurking our way, and yelled, but no one paid heed, or took him seriously. As a result of that, Côte d'Ivoire has fallen back in the fifties with a series of coups d'état experienced since 1999. President Gbagbo foresaw the mess we are in today, so he prophesized to the Ivorian people. I agree that God reveals hidden things to His Prophets, and wisdom is bestowed on only one person for the edification of a whole nation. Nevertheless, the calamities have finally reached our door exactly as President Laurent Gbagbo anticipated. Therefore, wouldn't it be nice today for the Ivorian politicians to see where they wronged and what they failed to see, then come to their senses and mend their ways? Then join their brother President Gbagbo, and together fix the mess? I am personally flabbergasted to see the same politicians, who created these problems, refuse to acknowledge their mistakes. Instead they have joined hands to plunge our country in a hollowing crisis. What is more galling is that the same are blaming President Gbagbo for being the problem, and the obstacle for the recovery of the country. This is nothing but the fruits of ignorance.

Alassane was imposed to Houphouët as a condition to get help from the IMF. He had no other alternative but to agree on the terms and condition of the loan, not knowing that behind all this was hidden Chirac's plan to install Alassane as the next President of Côte d'Ivoire. He knew that Houphouët would not survive another 10 years due to his advanced age. Unfortunately this plan failed, and his dream of re-conquering Côte d'Ivoire was shattered in 1993 when Konan Bédié took advantage of the Chapter 11 of the old constitution to self proclaim himself as the President of Côte d'Ivoire. Bédié then knew how important an asset the constitution of the country was.

Ignorance is a great danger; it is the worse enemy of mankind. One may possess the highest degrees in the world, but if he befriends ignorance, he may turn out to be a public danger, and lead a whole nation into chaos and confusion. For example, the Ivorian people said nothing in 1993 when Bédié self-proclaimed himself as President utilizing the constitution. In 2006, the same is rallying to have it suspended, and none of his supporters ever reminded him that it was the same constitution that made him President.

In 2005, the mediator in the crisis, his Excellency President Thabo Mbeki obtained the candidacy of Alassane Dramane Ouattara from President Laurent Gbagbo through the article 48 of the constitution.

A few months later, Alassane strongly requested the suspension of the constitution through which he obtained eligibility, and none of his supporters, or members of his cabinet reminded him that if his requested of suspension yielded, it might affect his candidacy for the election. The crisis in Côte d'Ivoire has become disconcerting, almost untreatable because of the above behaviors of the protagonists. They do not know what they want. None of them is reasoning intellectually. This leaves people like me astounded.

Without further analysis, we know what their problem is: they are troubled by the presence, wit, and wisdom of President Laurent Gbagbo. They merely want him out because he poses a threat to their culture of looting the country.

Well, for your knowledge and information, we are at a point where we will not let you have your way because we have the right to protect our country, even though we know that you will continue to fight us.

Chapter Seventeen:
General Robert Gueï
Leading the Military Transition in Côte d'Ivoire

GOD ALMIGHTY WHO POURS RAIN over all creatures; righteous or unrighteous, and blesses whoever it pleases Him to bless, gave General Robert Gueï this wonderful opportunity for two reasons:

First, God decided in His divinity to rehabilitate him after he was literally humiliated by President Bédié who wrongfully accused him for plotting to kill him. Bédié eventually fired him. This was a false accusation against him because General Gueï had always been known as a shy man, even under President Houphouët Boigny. We virtually never heard his name in connection with criminal activities. The truth of the matter is that dogs sometimes when they are frightened, bark at shadows of trees, or the wrong things. So Bédié lashed at General Robert Gueï for the wrong reasons.

Secondly, God decided to use General Robert Gueï as a source of inspiration, and a role model for the African. leadership, whereas someone tastes fame, glory and prestige, and still says:

"My fellow citizens, I am here today to speak to you about the political transition of our country. You know I took over at the beginning of the year to conduct the transition and lead our country to the Presidential election. I did my job for which God called me. Today the time has come for you to choose your President. As I promised to you in the beginning, I will not run for

President My job was to set up the guidelines for a democratic election and make sure that we minimize errors and frauds. Therefore I will be in power until the last day of the election, to validate the result, swear in the coming President, then step aside.
"

A typical example of such role model of leadership is former President Nelson Mandela of South Africa. He had a vision for which he fought all his life. He went to jail for twenty seven years. He came out and became the President of South Africa. After he did his term, he said: "I have achieved my goal. I have led my country where I wanted; out of apartheid, to freedom. I have done my job. I want my brother Thabo Mbeki to pursue my work." He is a hero today; and he will remain a hero even after he is gone out of this world. This is the level that we expect African people and leaders to reach. But sadly, the hunger for power is so high and crucial that they are ready to kill to maintain it.

When General Robert Gueï said the following, the whole world got a very good impression of him, and thought he would stand by his words: ***"I came to clean up the house in order to organize the election, and to allow the Ivorian people to choose whoever they want as their Leader,"*** he declared in his very first address to the nation and to the world. The whole world valued his manner and his way of thinking. Many called him [a man of integrity.] I guess he said that to put the Ivorian people to sleep, and then show his true identity later on. His first and only plan to which he succeeded was to give to the Ivorian people and to his country, a real constitution based on the realities of the time. To him, the old constitution was out dated, and inconsistent. This also was treasured by the Ivorian people, and also by the whole world. He led the referendum to ratify the new constitution. Thus, General Robert Guei started off well, with dignity until he begun tripping. When the world least expected it, he announced his candidacy for the presidential election, boldly contradicting himself. The world then started to lose trust in him. At one point, New York Times paper termed him as *"a man belonging to a tribe of men without* *character; who's yes is likely to mean No, vise-versa.*"

After the ratification of the new constitution by referendum, the General maintained his candidacy, and emphasized on the eligibility of potential candidates. According to the new constitution, any candidate who had had another nationality besides the Ivorian nationality was not eligible. Obviously, Alassane Dramane Ouattara was declared ineligible for having obtained more that one nationality; from his birth nationality, Burkinabé, to the American nationality, and now the Ivorian nationality. He was angry, but he did not express his discontentment publicly, or even fight back. Perhaps he respected the constitution; we assumed. Nobody understood why the [**Brave Tchê = Brave man**] kept quiet after being dismissed from the Presidential race.

Former President Konan Bédié on the other hand was the most unfortunate. He was in a voluntary exile in Paris after he was kicked out of office in 1999. He could not be counted as a potential candidate, therefore the two eligible candidates then were: General Robert Gueï, and President Laurent Gbagbo. Bédié probably felt frustrated in his place of Exile as the general did not mention him in the disposition of the election. I guess he never thought of coming back home, thinking he was still hunted down by the militaries. He probably blamed General Robert Gueï for his fate. I still wonder how Bédié could form such an alliance of Houphouëtists (Heirs of President Houphouët Boigny) with Alassane Ouattara in 2005, after calling him a non-Ivorian in 1995. How does Alassane become heir of Houphouët Boigny ten years later? This alliance of Houphouëtists with PDCI (Bédié) and RDR (Alassane) is a Union of Despair. It shows how incoherent are Bédié and the opposition at large. They are so desperate and controversial in everything they do or say. This unity alone can determine both individuals' level of political worthiness.

The Election Day on October 31ˢᵗ, 2000 was the bloodiest day ever experienced by Côte d'Ivoire, and the Ivorian people. At the end of the day when the (N.E.C) National Election Committee begun to announce the result of the Election by city and county, it was clear that the first ten ballots that were broadcasted were in favor of the candidate Laurent Gbagbo. While the proclamation of the result was in progress, the General appeared on TV, and announced the dissolution of the Election Committee, thus ending its operation. That same day he reappeared on TV to proclaim himself as the winner of the election.

This did not please the Ivorian people, especially the patriots who have demonstrated a high level of loyalty to their country since the time of crisis. They reacted vehemently, and massively moved toward the Presidential Palace where the general was with his spouse and his cabinet members at the time of the announcement. Soon, he was informed about the commotion. The General knew that his decision would spark anger and reaction, but he took chances to see if he would get away with it. We were later told that he courageously took the risk to honor his spouse, who put pressure on him, asking him to confiscate the power. What a strong lady she was? She probably said:
"Are you out of your mind to give the power to somebody else? If you don't want honors and privileges, I too want to be First Lady of this country."

This event should be a reference to whosoever is considering taking power any kind of way, to think twice. Our populations have been oppressed for so long that, they are no longer afraid to die when someone deprives them of their rights. They are willing to fight till the end, regardless of the consequences. Unfortunately, the General had one thing in mind that he downplayed the consequences. He even took things so lightly that he tried to intimidate the angry protestors. General Robert Gueï commanded his immediate guards to open fire at the furious protesters. And these ignorant guards executed his orders without a second thought. The more the guards fired at the angry protesters, the angrier they grew, and moved uncontrollably toward the Presidential Palace.

"General, we are in trouble," one of his body guards informed him.
"What is going on?" he asked the bodyguard.
"Our officers opened fire at them, but the more they do so, the angrier and furious the crowd gets, moving toward the palace. Honestly, if the bullets can not scare them away, who are we to stop them?" the guards said to him.
"*Donc, on fait quoi?* (Meaning) So what do we do?" he asked the guards.
"We are ordering a Helicopter for you and your family to escape," responded the guards.
"What about you guys," the general showed his concern.
"Don't worry about us chief; we will take care of ourselves," the guards responded and reassured him. Quickly, the general and his spouse boarded the helicopter, and fled in direction of Ghana, and all his staff disappeared in disarray, vanishing in the nature.

The election of October 2000, was not only marred by violence, but it marked the end of General Robert Gueï and the military transition in Côte d'Ivoire, from **January 1999, to October 31st 2000,** and sent the JUNTA to retire. After confirmation that the General had fled to an undisclosed location, the candidate Laurent Gbagbo spoke to the Ivorian people, asking them to stay calm. He then reinstated the Election Committee, and gave it back its original authority to resume the proclamation of the electoral result; which was fair to me.

In the end, there was no doubt; the result clearly favored Laurent Gbagbo, winner of the Presidential Election of October 2000. He was later sworn in as the new President of Côte d'Ivoire.

Chapter Eighteen:
President Laurent Gbagbo

HISTORY HAS ALREADY RECORDED all the acts undertaken by President Laurent GBAGBO in his life time, especially for his country; whether bad or good. History has bore records of all, and the satisfying part is that no one can change these records.

You may not like him out of jealousy for what he knows or for what he can offer to his country.

You may hate him because of the fact that he is politically more advanced than any politician in the country.

You may also despise President Gbagbo simply because he chose to do right by his people, and save his country from neo-colonialism; whereas his opponents chose to not only maintain the country where it was prior to the 60's, but they are even destroying what we have. You may disdain him for many other unspoken reasons; but the fact of the matter is that you do not have the chops to change him or make him act like you. Therefore, why wasting your time on things that you cannot change?

President Ggbagbo is unique. He is the only contemporary politician whom I know in Côte d'Ivoire, and I have seen to act with sense and think global, while others think individualistic. I can compare him to two great Biblical kings: King Solomon, for his wisdom, and King Hezekiah for his humility, and his fear of God.

Now, let me begin to highlight some of the actions undertaken by Laurent GBAGBO, and the risks attached thereof since he begun to contend President Houphouët Boigny. **First** of all, he broke the myth of the presidency of Houphouët Boigny. He contended him with the idea of Multiparty System. He literally challenged him. President Houphouët was so much offended that he tried to hurt him physically. At one point, Laurent GBAGBO had to escape from the country, and seek asylum in France. There were too much risks attached to the kind of vision he had. But this was something that he agreed to die for. You could see that he was called for a divine mission. He identified himself as the only fearful and respected opponent to President Houphouët Boigny. Some militants of the old party, PDCI hated him because he became an imminent trouble for the culture in place; while those who had discerned the purpose that drove him, and the opportunity he embodied, helped him escape the danger nightly. At that time no Ivorian could raise his finger to say anything to Houphouët Boigny, or even give him an advice on a specific matter, especially pertaining to political diversity. Every Ivorian in the country would know what I am talking about here. Whether you like Laurent GBAGBO or not, if you are true to yourself, you may not deny that he took those risks, not for himself, but to see his country liberated from an old dictatorial regime that was linked to the colonial system. Today all the Ivorian people have the privilege to express themselves freely, whether it is to insult the President verbally or in the newspapers or not. The truth is that today, they are able to acquaint themselves with freedom of speech. This is something that did not exist before. History has bore record of how we got to that point whether you like it or not. Since 1960, Houphouët Boigny had never faced an opponent during the Presidential election. He was always the only candidate against himself, and still, he was proclaimed winner at 98% of the election each time.

In 1990, thirty years later, the Ivorian people experienced

something in Côte d'Ivoire that had never been experienced, or even thought about before; and that was another candidate against Houphouët Boigny. The new candidate was Mr. Koudou Laurent GBAGBO; who went to the Presidential election with the aim to win or to lose, and not to serve as a crossing guard. He did not go in to play the role of a horse for the other candidate to ride on, or to serve for the legal purpose for the validation of his opponent's spurious activities. But he took the risks to take the power and send the old man to his retirement. In 1995, against Konan Bédié, it was a different ball game. During those elections, President Laurent Gbagbo demonstrated a high sense of responsibility as a well versed politician who does not do politics to accommodate others. He withdrew from the elections because after analysis, he discovered the sham and the machinations that were devised to guarantee Bédié's victory. So as a result, he called for an active boycott of the election. Bédié thereafter remained the sole candidate, thus facing a constitutional constraint. Democratically, there have to be more that one candidate for an election to take place. To cross over that hurdle, the old party did not lack ideas. So Wodié from the PIT party who was not initially a candidate for the election was pulled in to serve for the legal purpose. For the occasion, he became the second candidate against Bédié. I wonder if Wodié ever consulted his friends (the intellectuals), as they called themselves, before engaging his party in this election. Or could it be that they were simply so blindfolded by the hunger for power that it did not matter to them if they ruined their reputation in the process. Or was it that they did not care at all about what people might think about them? Here are people who call themselves (The party of the intellectuals), and went to help Bédié legalize his electoral fraud; that is amazing. Would an intellectual act without analyzing every situation deeply? Or could it be that they traded their integrity against money for the occasion? That may be a possibility. Money being the roots of all evil, it is why many enter politics in Africa to fill their pockets. This is the hollowing gap between the Ivorian politicians, and the kind of politician Laurent Gbagbo is. He came into politics with a vision that remained unflappable, sustained by an unflinching

determination. History has also bore record of that.
As **Bob Marley** sings: **"You can not fool all the people all the time."** The truth of the matter is that all you do, sooner or later will come back to haunt you.

President Laurent Gbagbo is the only Ivorian who stood in the face of Houphouët Boigny, and told him that the way he was governing the country was out dated. He is the only Ivorian politician that I know, who went across the country to educate people, telling them that the country needed to get out of slavery; the modernized version of it. He said in plain language that:

"The independence that we are celebrating every year is not a real independence; do not be fooled. The country is still crawling under the colonial yoke; so you are not independent. For instance when the country sells one kilogram of coffee or cocoa, the revenue is divided in this way: for $1.00 revenue, $0.15 comes to the farmers, $0.40 goes into the safe of the country, and the rest of the money, $0.45 goes into the safe of the colonizer, France. In this way can you say that you are independent? Until then, regardless how hard you work, you will never get what you are worth."

He spoke in a kind of language that even the illiterates could hear him, and taught the population that the time had come to reverse these practices. He is the only Politician who revealed the fictitious agreements that tied the country to France since the colonial era. *"How can a sea port be on the land of Côte d'Ivoire and be a French port?"* How can the natural water that God gave us to sustain a better living be French water? How can a building be built on the land of Côte d'Ivoire, and be leased from France? How can we be independent, and be restricted from purchasing our own goods from a foreign manufacturer? And whatever we purchase from abroad always have to transit in France before being shipped to Côte d'Ivoire with higher overhead taxes added to the original cost?"* he exclaimed. History has bore record of that as well.

Today, every child, woman, man and young man knows President Laurent Gbagbo. They know what his fight and his struggle are about. No one can deny it. He went through all this for the liberation of his beloved country. On top of that, he revealed his true intentions to his fellow Ivorian. Laurent Gbagbo's intentions were to be the President of Côte d'Ivoire one day, **through election**. No honest Ivorian can deny this. **"I will be the President of Côte d'Ivoire one day through election. The only way to be in power is through election,"** he said repeatedly to the Ivorian people during this educational campaign. He has never suggested any other way leading to the power, so let us be honest and give the man the credit he deserves. What then has he done wrong to deserve this treatment?

Note:

No one, including myself outside the government officials knows, and can say with precision the detailed content of the colonial contracts between France and Côte d'Ivoire, or any other country in Africa. So if any reader would ask me to provide proof that we are paying 65% of our yearly revenue to France, or bring receipts of rent for the Presidency and National Assembly Palaces paid to France, I will not provide them. However we know for sure that the colonial contracts that were written contained for the most parts some irregularities, repressive, and subversive clauses just for the benefit of the colonizer. And because of these improprieties, our countries with brittle economies are stifling. We also know for certain that the relationship between African countries and the colonizers has not been straightforward, nor was based on rationale. The colonizers wrote these contracts for their own benefit and interests. Today, our struggle entails the normalization of this relationship, and the freedom of our countries, so that we can develop ourselves without constraint of any type, shape or form.

Chapter Nineteen:
Making Peace: **President Laurent Gbagbo**

WHEN IT WAS ALL OVER, AND PRESIDENT LAURENT GBAGBO
made his first TV appearance to speak to the Ivorian people, we all
exploded in joy. "Our hard work has finally paid off," we said
assuredly but tepidly, with the aftermath of the violence that
erupted during the election, still lingering in our minds.

Because of that, and many other reasons, my joy did not last long
before it evaporated, leaving me in a state of perplexity. It simply
went off like a candle light. This literally happened to me for two
major reasons:

1- When President GBAGBO took office in October 2000, he
spent nearly a year trying to reconcile all the children of the
country. He wanted to build on the right thing: trust, and
forgiveness. This initiative was of good will. He wanted to unite all
the children of the country so that they could all dwell under one
roof and express love for one another. He literally delayed the
event, waiting for former President Bédié, and former Prime
Minister Alassane Ouattara who were playing on the conditions of
their safety. The two men postponed their arrival several times as if
President Gbagbo was the cause of their status of asylum, and for
the security breach in the country.

People create circumstances for their convenience, and
when these circumstances get out of hand and control, other people
who knew nothing about them get the blame. For instance,

Alassane Ouattara planned to create his own guards service in anticipation of becoming the President of Côte d'Ivoire. So he brought in the "Dozos," traditional hunters from Burkina Faso and Mali, and armed them illegally. When things did not go his way, these men were not disarmed, but mingled with the civilians. We heard words of the state of insecurity and crimes in the streets of Abidjan. Bédié on the other side recalled his wrong doings, and dwelled on the fact that the militaries would still be hunting him down since he was ousted from power. Now when both men received President Gbagbo's invitation for the reconciliation program, they raised the issue of their safety, holding President Gbagbo responsible. Bédié raised a second condition. He wanted President Gbagbo to renovate his house in Abidjan before coming. I knew they were both playing games with him and with the Ivorian people. Ironically, Bédié and Alassane Ouattara were only two people who were pulling us by the nose, so to speak, out of twenty plus millions Ivorian; think about it.

When finally all their conditions were met, they arrived. The reconciliation ultimately took place without reaching the expected goal. Instead, it turned out to be a platform of propaganda for Bédié and Alassane. They both teamed up later with other partners to organize a coup d'état to overthrow the Good Samaritan who brought them back home and shielded them. Even though they failed, they still have succeeded in creating confusion in the country, and rendering his term chaotic. The satisfactory part though is that: "One way or the other, we end up paying for what we do to others, especially those who have been good to us," no one gets away with that; that is a law of nature. In other words, the idea of reconciliation was a bright one, but the enemy's goal was to make President Gbagbo feel as if he made a mistake.

I recall one statement made by President Gbagbo on one occasion: **"There are some mistakes that you can not afford to make in politics because they can cost you,"** he asserted. Based on his own saying, the first thing he needed to do right after he was elected was to speak to the Ivorian people during the reconciliation, and begin working on his program without wasting time. The behavior of Bédié and Alassane proves today that the President made a fatal mistake (even though he didn't) for bringing them back home. They have both teamed up against him.

2 - I disapproved the first government of the FPI when President Gbagbo took office, because it was composed of 38 Ministers. I did not agree with the idea for the simple fact that I recalled some of the complaints of the opposition during the time of Houphouët Boigny. The opposition bitterly criticized him for forming a government of 40 Ministers. At one point he was dubbed; "Alibaba and the 40 thieves."

To this criticism, I agreed even though the opposition did not make any suggestion as how many ministers were appropriate for a government. Even though the critics were vague, I still agreed with the opposition, based on the testimony of John in the Book of Revelation. I believe in the testimony and the description of John on the pattern of an earthly government.

Revelation 1: 9, 10

"I John, ….. was in the isle of Patmos for the word of **God**, and for the testimony of **Jesus Christ**.

10- I was in the Spirit on the **Lord's Day**, and heard behind me a great voice, as a trumpet …….."

Revelation Chapter 4: 1-4

"After this I looked, and, behold, a door was opened in heaven: ….talking with me saying:…...*Come up hither, and I will shew thee things which must be hereafter.* **2-** And immediately I (John) was in the spirit; *and behold, a throne was set in heaven, and **One** sat on the throne.* **3-** *And He that sat was to look upon like jasper and a sardine stone: and there was a rainbow round about the throne, in sight like unto an emerald.* **4-** *And round about the throne were four and twenty (**24**) seats: and upon the seats I saw four and twenty (**24**) elders sitting, clothed in white raiment; and they had on their heads crown of gold.*"

These twenty four elders around the throne represent a true government, with God as the President, and his twenty four elders as Ministers around him. That is exactly the representation of a government on earth likely to remain in the fullness of God, and reflect His Glory. When a government is composed of 25 Ministers or more, it is likely to fail because it has unconsciously and automatically withdrawn from God's divine principle. It is possible to have less than 24 Ministers, as long as you do not exceed the figure 24. So I dauntlessly agreed with the critics of the opposition.

How the opposition could come in power a few years later to form a government composed of 38 Ministries, as opposed to the scolded 40 Ministers of the government of Houphouët Boigny? Out of the 38, some did not stand out. They could simply be merged with others in order to ensure worthiness, and effectiveness. And as a developing country, bureaucracy is not a tool for development.

I would never imagine the opposition coming to power one day and doing the very thing they repudiated in the past. There is a danger when you vilify something, and you turn around and do the same thing. This alone can trigger bad luck, sometimes curses, and it can hold you back. This is what whetted my sadness.

It transpired later that he, (the President) wanted to satisfy his long time and faithful friends in the struggle.
Although this was logically a compassionate idea, it was unfortunately non conformant with the Idea of re-foundation. When you want to re-found a country, you eliminate bureaucracy. You create new chapters to be targeted such as; goals, results to be reached, and a time frame to reach these goals. You also create opportunities to involve all the human resources available, whether inside or outside the country to bring in the new tools and the technologies required to implementing underground systems. Pleasing one's friends and companion in struggle is not a bad thing, but the compilation of both the inside as well as the outside resources is essential for the idea of re-foundation.

The re-foundation is a package that requires manpower,

skills in various aspects, and new technologies that can be applied in each chapter comprising the package. The exclusion of one can lead to the failure of the whole process. The friends alone without the outsiders who have the skills and the technologies can not do it. Nor the outsiders with the skills without the friends can either. In all things, a balance sheet is not an option.

Shortly after the first government was formed, a breach of trust grew among the President and his so-called friends, and betrayal surfaced in their midst. The President became the victim. He trusted his friends so much that the thought that some would betray him never haunted him.

Many are the friends who grew the wrong desires and simply positioned themselves where they belonged in first place. From Dakoury to many others, to the recent case that stroke me. Who would have believed that the well respected Chief of Staff of the National Army, Mathias Doué could barter his high ranking position to finally team up with the very rebels who turned many villages in the West, including his own into sinking waste lands? This would never have occurred if Mathias Doué did not grow the wrong desires.

I do not have the chops to paint the psychological nuances of politics and leadership in the African society. All I can say from this is that grimness shapes the panoramic range of rationale and politics in Africa. I am not concerned about what is happening elsewhere. Doué Mathias who saw his village destroyed by the rebels, found himself in Burkina Faso eating and drinking with the same rebels. He has been making lofty declarations ever since, and promising to attack to overthrow President Laurent Gbagbo. An intelligent person can find this unimaginable and badgering. I have no answer to it. That is why I suggest that the Ivorian people in particular, and the African leaders in general seek the face of **God**, and partnership with **Jesus Christ** so that they can perceive the Light, and be inspired to lead our continent out of the concave.

Until then, the few who are enlightened will continue to be

the victims of deep injustice. That is why President Laurent Gbagbo who is a true patriot, and believes in the freedom of his country is encountering hardship with his opponents in Côte d'Ivoire. They obviously do not speak the same tongue, nor share the same values.

Chapter Twenty:
What a tragedy

OUR **BEAUTIFUL COUNTRY**, Côte d'Ivoire has fallen low. A once very prestigious country is now straining to cope with the aftermath of a foiled coup d'état that have lead the country through five years of turmoil. We have always thought that in order to make it in life, we needed to go school to acquire education and skills; and that is exactly what we did. Many of the children of Côte d'Ivoire, and Africa have achieved a great deal of knowledge through education. Unfortunately, their dreams of succeeding in life are shattered by the behavior of selfish politicians, which produces atrocities of all kinds. Unemployed, but very devoted, they are the ones giving their chests to defend the interests of their countries from the oppressors. Most of the patriots in Côte d'Ivoire are jobless, while rebels are promoted to Ministerial positions, giving out the wrong impression that education nowadays is worthless. All you need to do is take weapons, terrorize, kill innocent people, and you will make it in life. **What a tragedy for our country?** I am praying that the powerful hand of the **Lord Jesus** lies upon his children; the patriots, so that none of them get negatively influenced by the above assertion. **[Weapons do not make anyone succeed in life.]**

You may get to the top by using weapons; remember that this is the devil's way of getting there. You will surely fall sooner or later because it was not **God** who placed you there. We have found ourselves in a country where anybody gets up in the morning to do or say what they want to do or say without being questioned, or being charged for the sake of Freedom of Speech, and Peace.

Freedom of speech for which President Laurent Gbagbo and his party fought, does not entail bad tongue; or disrespectful conducts; but intellectualism and maturity. Freedom of Speech was never achieved easily. Other people risked their lives to make things possible for all of us. They had a vision and a dream, and fought until this dream became a reality. Today we are in a multiparty system, and we have Freedom of Speech as a result of their hard work. Therefore, we the beneficiaries have to use these opportunities wisely and maturely. We should not take them for granted and abuse them. We need to look back and not forget the time we did not have these things. One terrible tragedy is when people forget their own history.

Freedom of Speech is not a runaway train that lost its track, and that has no known direction. Freedom of speech is neither a free fall when you ignore whether you are going to land upside down on a rock, or in rubble of steel. Freedom of speech has guidelines, and a direction. Those who don't remember how this freedom of speech came about are misusing it. How in a civilized nation, someone can, in a speech on National Television call partners and investors to discontinue all transactions with our country, and get away with it? The same called his fellow citizens to stop paying taxes, and have a disrespectful attitude toward their nation and their government, and still got away with that.
Oh! What a tragedy to see such things happening to us.

The whole class of politicians of the opposition has lost all senses of intellectual reasoning. In Elementary schools we learn what constitutes the basic of the sovereignty of a nation. Here are politicians who have no clue about what a constitution represents for a nation. In Côte d'Ivoire they are unanimously rallying for its suppression. I wonder if someone told them that their birth certificates would be suppressed or rendered invalid, how they would feel. They are all losing it over the philosophy of President Laurent Gbagbo.

I heard Konan Kouadio Bertin (KKB) say in a radio address that: "**I don't understand why they want to break free from France, when we speak the French language.**"
My question to this fellow is:
"Does the fact of speaking the French language put us in a state of permanent servitude? Does it give the French marines the right to kill our children, brothers and sisters? Did we steal the French language so now we have to pay for it with our lives? How much do we owe for speaking that language? So that we may adjust our budget in order to clear that debt once for all to avoid deferring it over our children and grand children after we are gone."

This is what we have to put up with in our country, and in Africa. Some people don't understand that we deserve freedom just because we were colonized by the white man of France. **This way of thinking** is a tragedy for the continent of Africa.
Another tragedy is when in a country like Côte d'Ivoire, or elsewhere, the law is silent, and the justice system is non-existent. Instead of in a nation that deserves respect, we tend to find ourselves in a jungle where the tough ones survive, and the weak ones are crushed.

As a child of **the Most High**, seeing my country fallen to such a degrading level, I can only glorify **His** name because I surely see my country within His principles: "Humiliate yourself, and **He** will lift you up." In other word, in order to be lifted up, you have to touch down. You have to fall first, and then **He** will raise you up. When you are already standing, there is no need for **Him** to lift you up from the ground. You have to touch the ground before you can be lifted up. So I only glorify **His Holy Name**, for I see Côte d'Ivoire being lifted up, and being an opportunity for the Ivorian people as well as for the entire continent of Africa; an opportunity to break free from the yoke of French colonialism, and neo-colonialism.

Chapter Twenty One:
Chirac is pursuing President Gbagbo

SINCE SEPTEMBER 19th 2002, after the failure of the coup d'état that was meant to overthrow him and keep him in exile, President Gbagbo was thus placed under close watch, in a red zone, so to speak. Every one of his steps and movements would be then followed, and every action he would take would be scrutinized, and misinterpreted.

During all the meetings and peace talks, the Ivorian government was conspicuously held culprit, and President Gbagbo and the Ivorian delegates were treated as if they were the ones who attacked Côte d'Ivoire, while the rebels were cherished. Almost like when **Jesus** stood in arraignment court, accused of all unimaginable crimes he did not commit. In fact the devil, the judges, Caïaphas the high priest, and Pontus Pilate the Governor, all knew that Jesus committed no crimes. They also knew that he was sent by God to save humanity, even though they pretended he wasn't. Therefore, they thought that by killing him, the mission for which he was sent would never be fulfilled. That is why they pushed forward with the crucifixion of Jesus Christ, in order to obliterate his mission once for all.

So by judging him with a guilty verdict, they thought they washed their hands clean. Physically speaking, it was a scene of injustice, very obvious to any naked eye; but at the same time, above all, there was "**the Divine purpose of God for humanity,**" which was oblivious to all, including satan.

Every situation is always shaped by two aspects:
1- The physical aspect which is visible to human eyes. This aspect is the source of polemics whereby each commentator thinks that he or she detains the truth, and his or her explanations and views are without blemish.
2- The Divine aspect; which is unknown to human wisdom. This aspect entails **the purpose of God in that particular matter**.

In the case of Côte d'Ivoire and President Laurent Gbagbo, the plans of men for him are to oust him from power; and the peace talks and all those meetings, accords and resolutions are a way of narrowing people's attention down on the fact that they are helping to restore peace. But when you look at things closely, you can tell that they are procrastinating, buying time, protracting the sufferings of the Ivorian people, distracting the whole world, setting up pits and stratagems to have him trapped in. Their ultimate goal is to end his reign.
The injustice against President Laurent Gbagbo and the Ivorian people is so obvious and so bold that I ask myself myriad questions. I particularly ask myself; what is it about this small country, Côte d'Ivoire that it is drawing so much envy and jealousy from its neighbors? What is so special about it that France, the former colonizer wants to re-conquer it, and own it so badly? There must be something special about it that drives them so crazy. They know the causes of the present condition of Côte d'Ivoire but they simply refuse to acknowledge it. What is happening to us is surely devastating and horrendous, but let us not be blown away by it, for the simple reason that above all things, there is an unshakable purpose for the Ivorian people in this crisis, which is unknown to human:
"The Divine purpose of God for the people of Côte d'Ivoire, for President Laurent Gbagbo, and our continent; Africa."

It is no secret today that Chirac and all his allied have converged together to crucify President Laurent Gbagbo. Because they do not find a way to topple him, they picture him as the "obstacle" *that thwarts them from reaching their goal*; not the obstacle to the peace process they are referring to. The peace process came about after they failed to overthrow him, so it is irrelevant to even mention it.

They have decided that they want him dead, after they have done every possible thing; from coups d'états to Marcoussis; politically and diplomatically to strip all powers from his hands without success. After they unsuccessfully involved the UN to write resolutions to override the country's constitution, they are desperate today. The ironic part is that these politicians and intellectuals have literally put aside politics, and have chosen to act like criminals and arsons, burning down entire buildings.

To this point, they have decreed that, it would no longer matter if Laurent Gbagbo had to die along with other heads of states. They hate him so much that they don't even want him alive. This is so cruel. In regard to this behavior of terrorism, the Ivorian people expect President Gbagbo to be firm and take actions accordingly as a President would. For instance, they would have hoped to see their President ordering a criminal investigation about the fail coup of **September 19ᵗʰ 2002**, to officially determine who the instigators behind it were. Then possibly issue an international arrest warrant against the criminals; instead of assuming that *we know who did this*. A criminal can remain innocent as long as he hasn't been indicted and sentenced.

List of events:
1- Concerning the event of **November 2004**, Chirac should have been prosecuted and brought before the International Tribunal in the Hague for genocide against young people with bare hands. This alone can constitute a precedent for a rupture of diplomatic relations.
2- In the month of **June 2005**, I believe, while the President was on his way to Abuja, nine French marines with the same weapons

as the Ivorian army, were spotted by a farmer at the end of the runway of the airport. Had the farmer not been vigilant, it would have been a disaster. He hastily alerted the Airport Authorities, and the President's plane was grounded.

The mission of these nine criminals was to blow up the plane of the President to make believe that his own militaries had killed him. People like these needed to be jailed, and sentenced.

When everything is fine, politics and diplomacy are tools to rule and manage state affairs. But when things are reversed, and you are dealing with people who have chosen to act like terrorists, burning down entire buildings, and looking for ways to destroy you, you need to change your attitude and be more firm. Not saying anything or taking any action for the sake of doing politics does not guarantee your safety either. Or not reacting for the sake of peace is not the right idea. Instead, you are exposing yourself unduly.

3- On **July 26, 2006**, at a meeting in Liberia, four Presidents: President John Kufuor of Ghana, Ellen Sirleaf Johnson of Liberia, the only lady President in Africa, Laurent Gbagbo of Côte d'Ivoire, and Ahmed Tejah Kabah of Sierra Leone, almost got consumed by fire. Right after the departure of then Sierra Leone President, the building where the meeting was held was set on fire, after someone turned off the lights. It was a tragic moment. Owing to the Ivorian security team, the three Presidents were able to escape unscathed.

A French helicopter hovered above the scene to fake a rescue, but no one yielded to its request. As an analyst, I concluded that the purpose of this rescue mission attempted by the men in the helicopter was to capture the four Presidents in case they would escape the fire, and take them in a remote and undisclosed area, and slay them physically, and then bring their bodies back into the blaze to be consumed. Had this terrorist operation been successful, Chirac would have been zestfully tearful while sending condolences to the people of Ghana, the people of Côte d'Ivoire, and to the people of Liberia, and possibly of Sierra Leone, then go behind the curtain to celebrate on Champagne for having reached his ultimate goal. For the three others Presidents, they would simply rule out that: "they were at the wrong place at the wrong time."

This was another victory of President Gbagbo over the notorious terrorist.

All this was happening in the full knowledge of the international opinion, but no one mentioned any of these events. Logically, it would be wise to expect an investigation of the UN to determine what happened while three prominent heads of States were in danger. But I believe that we will never see such a thing since Kofi Annan the Ghanaian, and Chirac's friend, is still at the head of the organization.

4- In the month of **August, 2007**, a ship called Probo Koala dumped chemical waste in the Abidjan, Capital City of Côte d'Ivoire. A group of Ivorian people received 17 billions FCFA to allow the dumping of the waste. In the investigation, two French men (related to Chirac) were detained in custody. Consequently, 10 people died, and 2500 others were intoxicated. This was nothing but an attempt to a mass murder of the Ivorian people. Their ultimate goal was to stir the anger of the population against President Laurent Gbagbo so the French troops could take advantage of it.

5- The Secretary General of the UN, Kofi Annan invited President Laurent Gbagbo to New York on September 20th 2006 for a meeting with all the parties involved in the crisis. At the same time, the 61st session of the UN was scheduled to take place. While all awaited, President Gbagbo cancelled the trip on the ground that he had enough of unproductive meetings and negotiations.

My son called me to ask my view point about the President's decision. I told him that he was right, and that I supported every decision he made. That same day, as the Prime Minister of Thailand, Mr. Thaksin Shinawata left home to attend the meeting at the UN, he was ousted by a coup d'état. When he arrived in New

York, Kofi Annan denied him access to the UN. The poor man just went back to his hotel room, and later flew to London where he has a house. **God** revealed this to show us what was planned against President Laurent Gbagbo, and what they were going to do to him once in New York. We could see that the more Chirac pursued him, the more he failed. We could see that **God** was his shield.

That is why I am taking this minute to reassure the Ivorian people, and especially the young patriots, to remain calm because the battle has changed venue. It is no longer our battle. I believe that President Laurent Gbagbo is well aware of the concerns of the Ivorian people, and he knows what needs to be done. On the other hand, he wants to avoid any situation that would put the lives of the patriots in jeopardy. That is why it seems like he is not acting firmly.

Today the veil has fallen off the face of the real rebels who attacked us on **September 19th, 2002**. We have been able to identify them from bottom to the top. We would never have known them if the coup d'état of September 19th 2002 had succeeded as planned. Things would have been so fast that we would never have known against whom we were fighting.

•

On September 28th, 2006 in Bucharest, Rumania, I felt so sorry reading what Chirac said. I would imagine that a French man would speak in such a pleasant tone with a clear language sweet to the ears, as opposed to the rubbish he mumbled. You could tell he was in such a state of despair that all he said was a mumbo-jumbo.

Here is Chirac's speech at the meeting of Francophony in Bucharest, Rumania.

" There is no possible horizon for our world and for our Francophony without peace. The tragedy that has once again caused bloodshed in Lebanon reminds us strongly. We can not tolerate that in our family, discord spreads flames; citing Haiti,

Mauritania and Togo, where tremendous initiatives have been undertaken to bring about basis for a peaceful political life, as well as the Republic Democratic of Congo (DRC) that is engaged in the search for peace and stability. A comparable reconciliation is wanted for Côte d'Ivoire, this **superb** country that President Houphouët Boigny raised to the top of development and democracy, and that today knows atrocities that we know of. **Only open and final elections, based on renewed electoral and rigorous listing can allow this country to come out of the crisis**.

I put my trust in all the Presidents of the African Union in order to take the necessary initiatives during the meetings, in the respect of the traditions. I hope that the peace process supervised by the AU and the UN would lead, before the end of October, to the general election aiming at unifying the country divided in two since the coup d'état perpetrated by the rebels on September 19th, 2002. Persistent disagreements of the protagonists on the issues of updating the electoral listings, and the disarmament, as well as regular confrontations of their followers, have made this date impossible to hold the election," said Chirac.

I wonder if Chirac knows what peace means. When he ordered the slaughtering of the youths in November 2004, was that an act of peace? Who is responsible for the atrocities that Chirac is referring to in the supposedly "superb country?" The nine (9) French marines who were spotted at the airport on a mission to blow up the President's Aircraft; who sent them? Is that an act of peace? When he went to burn down a whole building in Liberia, wanting to kill fellow Presidents; was that an act of peace? At the mention of the word "discords spreading flames;" who is causing these discords? And who is igniting these flames. Rallying for the suspension of the Ivorian constitution is not only discords spreading flames, but an act of vandalism and terrorism. Chirac's ultimate plan is to take President Laurent Gbagbo out of power before he gets dismissed by the French people. Chirac should learn how to read signs so he could understand that he failed since day one, and now he is ultimately defeated. Because he can not read those bold signs, he will continue to pursue President Laurent

Gbagbo, and still fail, until the French dignitaries get fed up, and decide to impeach him for bringing shame to France.

France was known as a great and respected country, until he came in power. Chirac does not have the last word. Our Father in Heaven has the last word. He has hardened Chirac and his allies' hearts as he did to Pharaoh when he sent Moses to tell him to free his people. He hardened his heart to better hit him with plagues. So let us keep still, and see His mighty hand coming against Chirac and his allies, in the name of Jesus. After the failure in Liberia, what is next to the menu of attacks? Let us be vigilant, and not be distracted; I am warning you because Chirac is a dangerous man. So dangerous that he is capable of ordering a collective suicide of the Ivorian people with the conspiracy of our own brothers; so let us watch each other's back from now on.

Conclusion

I **AM SADDENED TO WATCH** politicians, the UN, and the AU deploying so much energy in Côte d'Ivoire, trying to find a resolve to a problem that is not new to a continent long ravaged by the fruits of evil: poverty, bloodshed, and all that derive thereof.

I am more saddened to watch them struggling to find "**Peace**" for the Ivorian People; **a fruit of the Light**, on one hand, while they are holding on elements deriving from the power of darkness: heavily armed rebels, on the other. Obviously, I have to tell you: "You are on the wrong channel," because **Peace** and **Unity** are not the fruits of the power of darkness. Rather, they derive from the **Power of the Light**.

Light antagonizes darkness; that is why when the light came, the darkness did not receive it. You should seek **the light** first, taking appropriate actions accordingly, and in the end you will struggle less in the process of finding solutions to whatever circumstances might be at stake. There are two opposing mechanisms and two kingdoms that function in life. Every human being's life on earth is sanctioned by these two invisible or Spiritual entities:

1- The mechanism of the **Power of the Light,** and the **Kingdom of the Most High God**.

Vs.

2- The mechanism of the power of darkness, evil, and the kingdom of satan.

When you activate the mechanism of the Power of the Light, you will certainly receive the fruits that derive thereof, such as: Peace, Healing, Unity, joy, etc. But, when you activate the mechanism of the power of darkness, you will undeniably receive the fruits that derive thereof, such as: rebellion, bloodshed, chaos, confusion, division, poverty, and so on. You cannot activate the mechanism of the power of darkness, like Chirac and his allied are doing in Côte d'Ivoire, and in Africa as a whole, and expect to reap the fruits of the mechanism of the **Power of the Light**. It does not work that way.

From my stand point, the kind of peace they are talking about, and that they are pursuing is a conditional peace. It is plausible that they are targeting one person: President Laurent Gbagbo of Côte d'Ivoire.

President Gbagbo is a Patriot; he is not the right kind of guy that Chirac wants as leader of an African country, or of a French colony, to be accurate, because in his mind, these countries will "**Forever**" remain French colonies. Without repeating myself, let me remind you that; the colonizer will never reverse the law to set you free; you have to claim your own liberty.

President Laurent Gbagbo is too advanced politically that he has become a threat to the advocates of ignorance. He is a "**Woody**," a man of the land who is ready to defend and protect his family, and be willing to burn with it when his house is on fire and his children can not be saved; *"What good is it for me to live when my children are in the fire, helpless,"* kind of guy.

In other words, as long as he remains in power, they, Chirac and his allies will hold on tight to their rebels, buying time while they are looking for ways to accomplish their evil goal, treating President Gbagbo as the sole obstacle of their peace process.

If Chirac and Kofi Annan decide to disarm the rebels today, it will happen within twenty four hours; but they have decided that they will not disarm them until they have reached their goal. This is the game plan.

The UN troops and French Licorne had an agenda, presumably, when they were deployed in the country. Did that agenda include [the dissolution of the National Assembly?] I do not think so. Visibly, they started to play with the minds of the Ivorian people, and trying to create a state of confusion in order to blame President Laurent Gbagbo for it, and then justify whatever end result will derive from it, and use for in order to take him out. **November 2004** was Chirac's last opportunity: "Now or never," he said to his commander in chief leading the Licorne troop in Côte d'Ivoire. He was also sure of getting the undivided support of America with his alibi. Praise the **LORD** he did not. Côte d'Ivoire is a small country that has made France producer of coffee, when coffee does not grow on its soil. Côte d'Ivoire is a small country that contributes to the welfare of France in many aspects. It deserves respect, so we are determined to impose that respect to anyone.

We, the Ivorian patriots are determined to break the backbone of the French colonialism in Côte d'Ivoire. At the same time, we are ready to pay the price that comes along with our freedom.

Therefore, *you do not have to like him. He is the President of Côte d'Ivoire, and of the Ivorian people; not the President of France. So, as long as God loves him, and his people love him, it doesn't matter who does not like him.*

Conclusion:
Letter to the AU, and the UN.

BEFORE I CONCLUDE, I would like to bring three very important points to the attention of the **AU (African Union)** and the **UN (United Nations):**
1- Your involvement in the Crisis in Côte d'Ivoire.
2- Your decision to extend President Gbagbo's term,
3- The presidential Election.

1- Your involvement in the crisis.
Since your involvement in the crisis of Côte d'Ivoire, you have never spoken firmly to the rebels concerning all the killings and violations of human rights, and also their inconsideration for legality. Rather you have been very judgmental and prejudicial with the Ivorian government, and the young patriots who protect the interests of their country, and the President of Côte d'Ivoire, his Excellency President Laurent Gbagbo, portraying him as the obstacle of your peace process. **2- Your decision to extend President Gbagbo's term.**
    While the Ivorian opposition was groundlessly proclaiming constitutional void prior to October 2005, you jointly decided to extend the term of President Laurent Gbagbo by one more year. We did appreciate that. Thank you very much. However, at the same time you gave us the impression that legally, whenever a Presidential Election fails to take place in a country due to unusual

and hampering circumstances; the President has to step down to give his seat to anyone who desires it. You also gave the impression that President Laurent Gbagbo is to blame for the election not taking place, implicitly legitimizing the rebels who are obviously the cause of the hampering circumstances, and approving of the actual condition of the country.

3- The Presidential Elections.

While making this decision to extend his term, I believe that you laid down comprehensive plans, and you set reachable goals in terms of solving this issue before engaging in the election process. During this transition period, we expected that you might consider the following steps to reach the ultimate result of organizing the Presidential election, such as:

A- Disarming the rebels,

B- Unifying the country, then the other steps would follow, such as:

C- Preparing the voters registration,

D- Potential candidates, and campaign,

E- Election day.

As of August 3rd, 2006, two months prior to the next Election Day, October 2006, the impression you are giving us is that you are overlooking the steps **A**, and **B**, keeping the rebels in place, well grounded, with the country divided in two, and still striving to impose the election on the Ivorian people. Logistically, you know it is impossible to organize elections in such a condition Côte d'Ivoire is in; a country with a legal government in the South, and a rebels' government in the North.

African Leaders, are you intending to develop your continent with the system of rebellion? Is this how you intend to come out of the third world? In which African country have you ever organized elections in these conditions? Give us just one example of a country where you have ever applied what you are imposing on President Gbagbo, and we will follow your instructions. You know very well that there are countries in Africa that have never seen what an election is, and still the President remains in power. What is it that, those who organized the coup d'état, and created this condition, refuse to disarm their rebels, and you put the blame on President Laurent Gbagbo? If you want the country to heal, be fair. I am urging you to look at the facts, and treat this issue with more objectivity before it gets too late. The Ivorian people deserve peace. They are tired of the killing, bloodshed and trauma they have been taken through since September 2002. Very soon we will be in October 2006 with the probability of the election not taking place due to your failure to disarm the rebels. You know very well that you can not ignore the problem of the rebels in the country forever, and expect Côte d'Ivoire to do well.

Therefore, comes October 2006, if you are considering to make a decision concerning the conditions of the country, let it be a wise decision. Because, let me remind you of one thing; any ill thought decision will make things worse for the country and the Ivorian people; make no mistake about it.
Thank you for your understanding.

A letter to the Ivorian opposition parties

I **WOULD LIKE** to bring two issues among many to your attention:
1- The massacres of the West and Center West.
2- Your constitutional emptiness prior to October 2005.

1- The massacres of the West and Center West.

During the recent past months, there have been accounts of vehicles transporting people from neighboring countries into the

Western and Central Western parts of the Country. This is not a fairy tale, but a true story. The Prime Minister Konan Banny is planning to distribute citizenship to those foreigners in those regions were so many Ivorian people have been slain during the rebels killing spree. The plan is to replace those slain by foreigners, and give them voting rights for the future Presidential Election. This is insane. These types of things can only happen in countries that refuse to be developed in this new millennium, with the support of the thieves, and the looters of our economies.

Citizenship is not given to anyone who migrates in a foreign country. I am sure that France does not distribute citizenship in the streets of Paris to any one who comes along; to my knowledge. You call yourselves Ivorian, and you are killing your peers to replace them with foreigners, as if you decided to create a brand new country at your convenience, substituting yourselves to the creator of all things; God Almighty. This is unimaginable. Côte d'Ivoire is not a "**No man's Land**," therefore I conjure you, and your Prime Minister to stop abusing our country and our people. The only intellectual reason I can think of is that you hate President Laurent Gbagbo so much that you are willing to destroy your country today to satisfy your lust. Have you thought about the consequences when this back fires at you a few years from now?
Have you thought of a fixture to this complex problem you are creating today? What kind of country you are turning Côte d'Ivoire into? Do you have any idea about what you are doing?
Amazingly, you have a very strange and weird way of doing politics. God is watching you; the world is watching, and the Ivorian people are watching you as well. Be prepared to reap the fruits of what you are sowing today in a near future.

2- Your constitutional emptiness prior to October 2005.

Prior to October 2005 you proclaimed a constitutional emptiness, asking President Gbagbo to step down. From this you gave the impression (**A**) that in a country whenever there is no election for insecurity reasons and hampering circumstances, the President has to step down. I am flabbergasted by this. We have never seen such a thing in Africa or elsewhere. You also gave us the impression (**B**) that President Gbagbo is the cause why we did not have the elections. You are not being fair. (**C**)The third impression you gave us is that you are the proprietors of Côte d'Ivoire, and because your tenant did not pay his rent, he has to leave your property. I would like you to note the following: The Ivory Coast is not the private property of a group of people, an ethnic group, a political party, the colon, less an individual.

Therefore, legally, no one has the rights here on earth or in heaven to ask President Gbagbo to leave office without elections. It seems to me that you do not know what to do at this point. Therefore I am taking the time to tell you what you need to do:

1- You thought that you would take the power with the help of the rebellion. You have failed.

Therefore have the courage to disarm them because they are useless for the development of our country.

2- As soon as you disarm them, we will all join efforts to unify our country to bring back safety. It is only at this point that we will start the election process. Besides the above, you are wasting your energy and the time of the Ivorian people.

3- The longer we will dwell in this predicament, the longer it will take us to ever move forward and act as civilized people. Suppose it was one of you in the seat of the Presidency right now, and for the same reasons we did not have elections, and we asked him to step down, I am sure you would probably treat us as fools, wouldn't you? Treat others the way you want to be treated. The way you are treating President Gbagbo your own brother, is not fair. Therefore, come to your senses, and act right in the wake of the recovery of our country.

He, who has an ear, let him hear.

Index

CôTE D'IVOIRE = IVORY COAST
The President of the country:
Excellency President Laurent Gbagbo

FPI - Front Populaire Ivoirien / Ivorian Popular Front;
This is the party of President Laurent Gbagbo, the party in power now in Côte d'Ivoire.

RDR - Union of the Republicans: Alassane Dramane Ouattara (ADO)'s party

PDCI - Democratic Party of Côte d'Ivoire: Henri Konan Bedie's party.

U.N - United Nations

AU - African Union

ECOWAS - Economic Community Of West African States

CFA Franc - The official currency of Côte d'Ivoire

Linas Marcoussis - Marcoussis is the database of The French injustice against Côte d'Ivoire; an accord written as the solution to the conflict.

43rd BIMA (Brigade of Maritime Infantry) the French Military base in Côte d'Ivoire.

adjehi@yahoo.com
Send your comment to the Author.

I will now leave you with the Psalm 27.

The LORD is my light and my salvation; whom shall I fear? The LORD is the strength of my life; of whom shall I be afraid?

2- When the wicked, even mine enemies and my foes, come upon me to eat up my flesh, they stumbled and fell.

3- Though an host should encamp against me, my heart shall not fear: though war should rise against me, in this will I be confident.

4- One thing have I desired of the Lord, that will I seek after; that I may dwell in the house of the LORD all the days of my life, to behold the beauty of the LORD, and to inquire in his temple.

5- For in the time of trouble He shall hide me in his pavilion: in the secret of His tabernacle shall He hide me; He shall set me up upon a rock.

6- And now shall mine head be lifted up above mine enemies round about me: therefore will I offer in his tabernacle sacrifices of joy; I will sing, yea, I will sing praises unto the LORD.

7- Hear, O Lord, when I cry with my voice: have mercy also upon me, and answer me.

8- When thou saidt, Seek ye my face; my heart said unto thee, Thy face, LORD, will I seek.

9- Hide not thy face far from me; put not thy servant away in anger: thou hast been my help; leave me not, neither forsake me, O GOD of my salvation.

10- When my father and my mother forsake me, then the LORD will take me up.

11- Teach me thy way, O LORD, and lead me in a plain path, because of mine enemies.

12- Deliver me not over unto the will of mine enemies: for false witnesses are risen up against me, and such as breathe out cruelty.

13- I had fainted, unless I had believed to see the goodness of the LORD in the land of the living.

14- Wait on the LORD: be of good courage, and He shall strengthen thine heart: wait, I say, on the LORD.

Be blessed, in the name of Jesus Christ.

Printed in the United States
140548LV00003B/175/P